#Brooketales

One Baby's NICU Story and a Mother's Healing Journey

KRISTEE HALL

Copyright © 2026 Kristee Hall

All rights reserved.

No part of this publication may be reproduced, stored in a retrieval system, or transmitted in any form or by any means—electronic, mechanical, photocopying, recording, or otherwise—without the prior written permission of the publisher, except in the case of brief quotations used in reviews or scholarly works.

Scripture Acknowledgment

Scripture quotations contained herein are taken from the **Holy Bible**, including the **New International Version (NIV)** and the **New King James Version (NKJV)**. All Scripture quotations are used by permission. All rights reserved.

Disclaimer

The views and experiences expressed are solely those of the author and are not intended to serve as medical, legal, or professional advice.

Publisher

The 1 and Only Publishing
4500 Forbes Blvd
Lanham, MD 20706
info@the1andonlypublishing.com
www.the1andonlypublishing.com

Editing, design, and publishing services provided by **The 1 and Only Publishing**.

ISBN

Paperback ISBN: **979-8-89741-045-3**
eBook ISBN: **979-8-89741-046-0**

Library of Congress Cataloging-in-Publication Data
A Cataloging-in-Publication record for this book has been applied for.

Printed in the United States of America

To my mother— the first woman who showed me what strength looks like before I ever had words for it. Thank you for your prayers, your patience, and the way you held hope when I could not. For standing steady when fear tried to take over, and for loving both my daughter and me through a journey none of us expected. Brooketales exists because of the foundation you laid— your faith, your resilience, and your unwavering belief that love carries us through even the hardest seasons. This book is for you. With all my love and gratitude.

— Kristee Hall

How to Use This Book

This book serves two purposes: It's my story, and it's a roadmap for yours.

If you're currently in the NICU: Each chapter ends with reflection questions and coaching notes designed to help you process your own experience. Don't feel pressure to read straight through—jump to the chapters that speak to your current situation.

If you're post-NICU: Use this book as a healing tool. The reflection questions can help you process trauma, celebrate victories, and find your voice as an advocate.

If you're supporting someone in the NICU: This book will help you understand what families face beyond the medical procedures—the emotional battles, systemic challenges, and quiet victories that rarely make it into conversations.

Remember: Your story matters as much as mine. Use the margins. Write your own reflections. Make this book a companion on your journey.

Contents

How to Use This Book v

Prologue: When Life Shifts Without Warning 1

Chapter 1: Breaking the Cycle 5

Chapter 2: When Everything Changes 15

Chapter 3: The System Behind the Curtain 25

Chapter 4: Fighting for Her Life 33

Chapter 5: Finding My Voice 43

Chapter 6: The Surgeries and Patterns That Made Me Question Everything 51

Chapter 7: The Long Road Home 63

Chapter 8: Life After NICU— The Real Beginning 77

Chapter 9: The Cost of Fighting and the System's Response 91

Chapter 10: Watching Her Bloom 105

Chapter 11: The Freedom We Fought For 113

Chapter 12: Home Sweet Victory 121

Chapter 13: Watching Her Grow Beyond All Expectations 135

Chapter 14: The School Years Begin 147

Chapter 15: Champions in the Making 161

Chapter 16: Survival Tips for NICU Families 175

Chapter 17: Faith, Fire, and the Future 185

PROLOGUE

When Life Shifts Without Warning

"Moreover, God is able to cause all his undeserved kindness to abound toward you so that you are always completely self-sufficient in everything, as well as having plenty for every good work."
— 2 Corinthians 9:8

Imagine feeling helpless as your body begins to reject the very life growing inside you. You did everything right—ate well, stayed active, prayed up, kept your stress down—and still, your water breaks out of nowhere. You can't stop it. You feel it running down your legs, and there's nothing you can do to hold it in.

That was me in February 2017. Alone. No spouse. No family around. Just me, surrounded by a flood of emotions I didn't yet have words for. Fear. Despair. Anger. Skepticism. Was my baby going to make it? Would she be healthy—or would she suffer lifelong complications from this sudden, traumatic turn? I was a brand-new mother, and this was nothing like what I had imagined. It almost felt like I was walking in my own mother's footsteps.

I, too, was born prematurely in 1978. My mother delivered me alone in an ambulance that had to travel more than fifty miles from Andrews Air Force Base to Georgetown University Hospital in Washington, DC. Unlike her, I was only five minutes away from the hospital where my baby girl—and my life—would become permanently intertwined. We were no longer two separate beings. From that moment forward, we were in this together.

I questioned everything.

- *What did I do wrong?*
- *Why is she coming in February instead of June 3?*
- *Did I do something to cause this?*
- *Am I undeserving of a healthy baby?*
- *Is this karma for something I did—or didn't do?*

The questions wouldn't stop. And none of them came with answers.

Statistics That Matter

Babies born at twenty-five weeks are considered "micro-preemies." They have a seventy-five to eighty-five percent chance of survival and typically require extended stays in the NICU. Women who were born preterm themselves have a higher risk of delivering preterm, even when other risk factors aren't present. Several studies also show that preterm birth can lead to increased risks of developmental delays.

During my daughter Brooke's NICU stay, I met other families—some stronger than they knew, some holding on by a thread. Some babies couldn't breathe on their own. Some couldn't eat or gain weight. Others were thriving, hitting milestones early. Some families were rushed to take their babies home too soon because insurance wouldn't cover more time. Some babies didn't make it. I cried with those parents. I prayed with them.

And still, my baby girl was there. Longer than expected. Time kept stretching. I kept asking, "When will she be released?" And in return?

Cold stares. Sarcasm. Shrugged shoulders. Every week, a new doctor. And every new doctor was just as confused as the last.

I held on to my routine: work, home to change clothes, a quick meal packed to go, then straight back to the NICU. My life revolved around that unit. The beeping, the alarms, the white coats rotating like clockwork—it became my world for ten months. Even at home, I could still hear the machines ringing in my head. Sleep? Barely. But none of that mattered. Advocacy was my job now.

I thought it would all get easier after her release. It didn't. Post-NICU visits came with new doctors, new questions, and the same odd energy. A family member in the medical field quietly mentioned that my file might have been flagged. A caseworker later confirmed it. Some would say I was being paranoid. I know better.

But no matter the whispers, no matter the shade—we beat the odds. My baby girl kept growing, developing, and shining. She was strong-willed. Smart. Sassy. Unapologetically herself.

There were angels in the journey, too. One doctor saw me—*really saw me*—and connected me with a home health nurse service. One of those nurses introduced me to a woman who became a close friend. Then came a daycare provider who didn't just watch Brooke—she helped her thrive.

These experiences—I now call them Brooketales—have changed my life in ways I'm still uncovering, one moment at a time. This journey birthed my purpose, carried me into a community I never knew I needed, and gave me the courage to say: *You're not alone.*

To every NICU family out there—I hope this story helps you feel seen. I hope it gives you the courage to tell your own.

Breaking the Cycle

"You shall not bow down to them or worship them; for I, the LORD, your God, am a jealous God, punishing the children for the sin of the parents to the third and fourth generation of those who hate me, but showing love to a thousand generations of those who love me and keep my commandments."
— Exodus 20:5-6

Before the baby, before the NICU, before the world learned the name Brooke Giselle Hall...

There was just me—Kristee. A woman who had it all together on paper: career, ambition, independence. But in my heart, I was still trying to heal from decisions I made long ago, dreams I had to bury, and the parts of me that felt undeserving of love.

A Southern Start and a Premature Arrival

I was born in Washington, DC, in December 1978, before the big snowstorm of February 1979. My mother was just twenty-one years old, spunky and full of life. She had moved to the big city from North

Charleston, South Carolina, and met my father—a military man from Columbus, Georgia—on the Navy Base. They were two Southern gems trying to make a life together in the North.

She used to laugh and say she didn't follow a single doctor's rule while pregnant with me. She lived life boldly.

When the contractions hit, my father was at work, and she was home alone. After two long hours on a bumpy ambulance ride, more than fifty miles to Georgetown University Hospital, she gave birth to me—two pounds, nine ounces.

I was small, but I was strong. I stayed in the hospital for two and a half months. My mom would visit and hold me in the palms of her hands. My father was scared—I was so tiny. But I made it home two months later, through nine inches of snow and into the arms of two young, determined, and vibrant parents.

The Climb to Texas

From a young age, I was driven. I built my career fast, starting in Washington, DC, with the Department of Commerce, then grinding through years of federal service until I was making nearly six figures before thirty-five. But after thirteen years in Maryland, I felt stuck and unfulfilled.

I thought a change of scenery might lead to a change in life. I applied for a Department of Human Health and Services job in Atlanta, but when they contacted my current supervisor for a reference, he wasn't supportive. The offer went to someone else, a close friend of mine.

I was devastated. But I didn't stay down for long. I saw a vacancy with the Department of Agriculture in Fort Worth, Texas. It felt drastic, but something told me to go for it.

I got the job. Moved. Reinvented myself. I left DC behind with the hope that maybe, just maybe, my future—my family—was waiting for me in Texas.

Him

We met in August 2014, right after I moved. Our relationship was... undefined. Off and on for three years. I wanted commitment. He gave inconsistency. The worst of it? I found out he had been seeing another woman *while living in my home.*

My heart broke quietly. But something about him wouldn't let me walk away. I craved the comfort of his presence, even when I knew it wasn't love. Or at least, not the kind of love I deserved.

The Night That Changed Everything

It was September 5, 2017—his birthday. After a long stretch of silence, we spent the evening together one last time. It felt different. Tender. He kissed my forehead, and something in me felt both peace and a strange unease.

Weeks later, I missed my menstrual cycle. I took the test. Positive.

Wrestling With the Truth

When I told him, he fell silent. Not a word. No congratulations. No joy. Just...nothing. And that silence echoed everything I had been afraid of.

I was thirty-eight. No children. Previous health issues. And a silent history of pain that lived deep in my spirit—a freshman-year abortion I had never fully healed from. I wasn't turning back. Not this time.

This baby was my redemption. My restoration. My chance to show Jehovah that I could honor the life He had entrusted me with. I had already sinned through fornication, but I wouldn't compound it with regret.

I didn't tell anyone at first. I carried the secret alone until I was three months along. I needed time to make peace with it. To pray. To prepare. To protect what little joy I had.

A Baby Girl and Big Dreams

The doctor confirmed it was a girl. Every time we saw her on the ultrasound, she was bouncing, flipping, and living her best life. I started dreaming again. I had always loved fashion and dreamed of modeling in Paris. I wanted to pass that grace and confidence to her.

Favorite names floated around—Brooklyn, Madison, Kendal. But one stood out: Brooke. Elegant. Strong. Beautiful. I paired it with Giselle. Brooke Giselle Hall. She sounded like a girl who could walk the runway and own the room—or command a boardroom, dominate the court.

At night, I would pray. I knew I hadn't done it the right way—but I also knew God saw my heart. I asked Him to keep her safe. I asked Him to forgive me. I asked Him to surround us with people who would do us good. I promised to live a better life. To raise her with love, structure, and faith. I was ready to step out of singledom and into motherhood. Not just as a title—but as a calling.

The Tale of Two Preemies
by Kristee Hall

Birthed not big, yet awfully small
Thought to be weaker and assumed to fall
Mother and daughter stood resilient and tall
to face this world, not knowing what obstacles and feats
faced them after all.

They are not the first but set the tone
for other NICU moms and families, as an example shown—
of strength, survival, love, fear, hope
and proven to brawl when given no rope.

With all faith in Jehovah and the courage of Jesus,
this mother and daughter duo
survived the NICU to tell the story,
to encourage all of the gift of life after ups and downs—
a true story of triumph and love!

Coach's Note

I LOOK BACK AT THIS PART OF MY LIFE AND STILL FEEL ALL the tension—the guilt, the hope, the silence, the dreams. I didn't have a perfect beginning, but I had a heart full of love and a mind set on doing better.

This chapter reminds me that healing doesn't erase the past. It allows us to own it, grow from it, and walk with purpose. If you've made mistakes, you're not alone. I'm right here with you. And if you're ready to turn your pain into something powerful, I pray my story gives you the strength to do just that.

- **What I needed then:** Permission to have made mistakes and still deserve love and motherhood.
- **What I know now:** Our beginnings don't disqualify us—they prepare us for what's coming.
- **For the NICU parent reading this:** Your past doesn't determine your capacity to fight for your child. Every mother has baggage, but what you carry can become your strength.

Chapter Reflections

Every mother has a beginning—and every beginning has baggage. But what you carry doesn't disqualify you. It prepares you. Your beginning wasn't perfect—but was it honest, intentional, and full of grace. That's the kind of soil miracles grow in.

CHAPTER REFLECTIONS

1. What "baggage" from your past do you need to reframe as preparation rather than disqualification?

CHAPTER REFLECTIONS

2. Where in your life have you experienced silence when you needed support? How did you find your voice?

CHAPTER REFLECTIONS

3. What promises have you made to yourself or your children about the life you want to build?

When Everything Changes

"So that we may be of good courage and say, 'Jehovah is my helper; I will not be afraid. What can man do to me?'"
— Hebrews 13:6

I've come to understand that motherhood is not for everyone. Having lived through its trials and triumphs, I deeply respect the strength it demands—and the grace it requires. The gift of motherhood doesn't only belong to biological parents. It extends to the village that surrounds a child, nurturing them in ways big and small.

I never expected the events that led to Brooke's birth. I always imagined myself becoming a mother, but I didn't know when—or how—it would happen. I was focused on advancing my career in the federal government. I didn't imagine being single when I had my first child. I felt conflicted. The traditional nuclear family was the model I saw and the life I once believed I was meant to build.

But life had other plans.

Over the years, I've realized that emotional connection—between mother, father, and community—is what truly matters most for a child's well-being. Brooke's father and I continue to develop a better co-parenting relationship, despite a rollercoaster past. This is our story—a testimony of survival, perseverance, and hard-won wisdom.

The Shift

The moment I found out I was pregnant, I was overcome with joy. My doubts about motherhood—about whether I had waited too long—were answered. At thirty-eight years old, I was scared, but I also felt the most beautiful I've ever felt. Carrying Brooke, even only for four months, was a defining moment in my life.

Still, life wasn't easy. I was juggling intense demands at work as an acting supervisor, managing a team of eight while handling high-stakes special projects that required sign-off from National Headquarters. The stress was mounting.

My final special project took the heaviest toll. I presented a comprehensive workflow process, only for 85% of it to be dismissed after a new policy was suddenly introduced. I revised everything, led a conference call, and by all accounts, it was a success. But I was exhausted—mentally, emotionally, and physically. I had been basking in baby apps and nursery plans—then, in a blink, I was on the phone with a maternal-fetal specialist.

The shift wasn't just medical; it was spiritual. I started praying in ways I never had before—not out of habit, but desperation.

The Emergency

I was twenty-five weeks pregnant when my world shifted from glowing anticipation to gut-wrenching uncertainty. What started as a routine ultrasound became a moment I would replay in my mind a thousand times. I didn't know it then, but the words I heard that day would change everything: "We need to run more tests."

That weekend in February, my life changed forever. I was laughing on the phone with my mother after a quick run to McDonald's when I noticed something unusual: heavy, clear discharge. I wasn't cramping, so I decided to wait and see.

I made calls to every mom I knew. Their answers were cautious: "Maybe...just wait until morning." But as the night went on, the discharge became heavier, and Brooke's kicks grew fainter. That was the alarm I couldn't ignore.

The next morning, I went to the emergency room. That decision may have saved Brooke's life.

At the appointment, I was told there was no amniotic fluid around her. She was breech—head up, hands waving in the sonogram—and my heart dropped. I felt helpless and completely alone. I had never heard of a baby being born at twenty-five weeks and surviving. The hospital could only support babies born at twenty-seven weeks.

I was placed on bed rest, hopeful I could hold on just a little longer. But while I was lying there—praying for time, trying to stay calm—chaos erupted around me.

Labor was already underway when everything stopped. One second, the monitor beeped steadily. The next, silence. My daughter's heartbeat vanished, and so did my breath.

Brooke started moving more, and the contractions came faster. I screamed for help. They gave me medication. And when I woke up, I saw a tiny, precious baby girl—born a micro-preemie. So delicate, yet so precious.

The Storm Within the Storm

I was barely awake when the doctors told me Brooke would need to be transferred to a different hospital for her care. I would remain behind to recover.

The chaos didn't stop. The nurses were inconsistent. Some didn't check on me at all. I felt invisible in a place where visibility should've been lifesaving. Every morning, someone from billing called to remind me about my deductible—while my child's life hung in the balance.

I was told I needed to visit her at the new hospital daily. But I was barely healed, scared, and without transportation. I was used to taking care of myself. Being dependent was unfamiliar and uncomfortable.

One day, I stepped away to change my clothes and grab a bite to eat—I was gone for maybe thirty minutes. When I returned, a nurse pulled me aside and told me I was being reported for "abandoning" my child.

I lived fifteen minutes away. I had checked in. But that didn't matter. She didn't ask questions—just assumed the worst.

I stood there in disbelief, then walked out and cried in the parking lot. I just sat there—windows fogged, hands shaking, unsure if I had anything left to give. I felt the weight of every prayer I had ever prayed crashing into silence. And then, with my hands trembling and my soul cracking—I whispered, "God…are You there?"

These weren't the medical emergencies people expect to hear about. But they were real. The emotional ambush of it all—the paperwork, the accusations, the silent treatment—it nearly broke me before Brooke ever got the chance to fight for herself.

Coach's Note

SOMETIMES, THE TRAUMA DOESN'T COME FROM THE DIAGNOSIS. Sometimes, it comes from indifference. From policies. From cold hands and colder stares. I didn't just survive the NICU. I survived being made to feel invisible, incapable, and unheard. For any mother navigating that same fog, know this: Your presence is power. Even when the room doesn't acknowledge it.

- **What I needed then:** Someone to see me as capable and inform me of what was really happening.
- **What I know now:** Being dependent doesn't make you weak—it makes you human. Asking questions isn't being difficult—it's being a mother.
- **For the NICU parent reading this:** You can be falling apart and still show up perfectly. Don't let anyone rewrite your story.

Chapter Reflection

You can be falling apart and still show up. You can be doubted by the world and still be right where you need to be. Don't let anyone rewrite your motherhood narrative—not even the experts.

CHAPTER REFLECTIONS

1. When have you felt invisible in a space where you deserved to be seen and heard?

CHAPTER REFLECTIONS

2. How do you distinguish between necessary vulnerability and harmful dependency?

CHAPTER REFLECTIONS

3. What systems have made you feel like an outsider in your own story?

3

The System Behind the Curtain

"He gives power to the tired one, and full might to those lacking strength."
— Isaiah 40:29

The NICU isn't quiet. People imagine rows of sleeping babies with lullabies playing softly, but that's not reality. It's a place of constant beeping. Alarms that dig into you. The steady hum of machines breathing for your child. The squeak of nurses' sneakers. The doctors' low murmurs in that tone that makes your stomach knot.

When you'd been there as long as I had, the sounds become like a second language. I could tell when an alarm meant "minor adjustment needed" versus "something's wrong." My heart rate adjusted itself to match the urgency in the room.

The First Warning

Brooke's first doctor was gentle when he told me about the tiny hole in her heart. "It's nothing to worry about," he said. "Many people live their whole lives never knowing they have one."

I nodded. I wanted to believe him. I clung to his tone.

But three months later, a new doctor walked in and said, "Ms. Hall, I believe it's in Brooke's best interest to perform surgery to close her heart, because the hole is now bigger."

"Wait. What?" I said. "I've been asking about her heart every week. Every nurse has told me there's been no change. How is it suddenly bigger?"

He avoided my eyes. "The echo taken earlier today showed the change."

No pictures for me to see. No opportunity for me to judge for myself. Just his word and my pounding heart.

Faith Before Fear

I called my mother. Then my aunt. Both reminded me—in the way only family can—that Jehovah hadn't brought us this far to leave us. By the end of those calls, my fear had been reduced to a sentence: *Jehovah, take care of my baby girl.*

The surgery was set for the following week. The doctor reassured me: "This procedure is common. She's in good hands."

She came out of surgery like she was proving a point. My baby girl was a fighter.

Then the clipboard came. A nurse handed me a form. "We'd like to include Brooke in a research study. No compensation, but it could help her thrive."

I scanned the paper. Words like *experimental prescriptions* and *no guaranteed benefit* jumped out at me.

"No," I said. "Absolutely not."

She pressed. I pressed back. I didn't carry Brooke for twenty-five weeks just to have her treated like a lab experiment. But I didn't know then that saying no might add months to our NICU stay.

The Switcheroo

After the surgery and my refusal, I noticed the changes. New nurses. New doctors. Faces switching so often it felt like musical chairs. At first, I told myself it was normal. But you know when something doesn't sit right in your spirit.

One evening, a nurse moved Brooke's incubator, and the lights went out. Every monitor. Every machine. Silence. After a few failed attempts to fix it, we were relocated to the far end of the NICU—what I call The Lonely Wing.

It was quieter there—too quiet. In the busier areas, nurses and doctors passed through constantly. In The Lonely Wing, hours went by without a visit. And I couldn't ignore what I noticed: Half the babies in that wing didn't make it. The air felt heavier. Brooke seemed to feel it too—she was restless, irritable, and rolled her eyes at the nurses.

Seven months in, a new diagnosis appeared out of nowhere: She had pulmonary hypertension. Not a single daily report had mentioned it before.

The Bigger Picture

It was around this time that I started to connect the dots—not just about Brooke, but about the NICU as a whole. Some babies went home quickly, even if they seemed more fragile. Others, like Brooke, stayed and stayed, with shifting reasons and vague explanations.

I later learned the statistics: Black infants are twice as likely to be born preterm compared to white infants. Very low-birth-weight preemies account for seventy percent of neonatal deaths—and most of them are Black. Disparities persist even *inside* the NICU—rooted in systemic racism and unequal care.

Knowing those facts is one thing. Living them is another. And in The Lonely Wing, I was living them.

I had learned Brooke's rhythms—how she liked to be held during feedings, the tiny flicker in her eyes before she drifted to sleep. When I stayed overnight, I made sure I was the one to feed her. She took every bottle without issue.

The doctor joked, "You should be a nurse."

"No," I told him. "I'm more than a nurse. I'm her advocate."

Because in the NICU, being an advocate is the difference between progress and delay, between trust and suspicion. And that was just the first fight. The next one would test me in ways I never imagined.

Coach's Note

Advocacy isn't about being loud; it's about being clear. In rooms where the answers wobbled, I learned to anchor myself in facts, faith, and *Brooke's actual behavior*. If something didn't add up, I paused the train: "Show me the image. Walk me through the numbers. Explain the plan."

That wasn't me being "difficult." That was me being *her mother*. If you're in a NICU, you're not just visiting—you're a part of the care team. Wear that truth like a badge.

- **What I needed then:** Permission to trust my instincts and ask hard questions without being labeled *difficult*.
- **What I know now:** Patterns tell stories that people sometimes ignore. Documenting what you see isn't paranoia—it's advocacy.
- **For the NICU parent reading this:** Your intuition matters. When something feels off, dig deeper. You know your child in ways the rotating medical staff never will.

CHAPTER REFLECTIONS

1. Where did your intuition whisper, "something's off"? Write down one moment and what your body felt like in that instant.

CHAPTER REFLECTIONS

2. List three specific questions you'll ask at your next appointment (e.g., "What changed since last week?" "Can I see the imaging?" "What is the discharge path and what milestones remain?")

CHAPTER REFLECTIONS

3. Note one way you can document patterns—because patterns tell stories that people sometimes ignore.

4
Fighting for Her Life

*"God is our refuge and strength, a help that
is readily found in times of distress."*
— Psalm 46:1

It started like any other workday—emails, check-ins, little fires to put out. My acting supervisor hat on, voice steady, my eyes scanning spreadsheets while my heart lived miles away in a room full of alarms and wires. Then my phone lit up with the hospital's number.

My stomach fell through the floor.

"Ms. Hall, this is Dr. _____. We...need you to come immediately. Brooke isn't responding."

Everything inside me iced over. "What do you mean—*not responding*?"

"We need you here to observe her condition."

I don't remember hanging up. I remember the hallway tilting. I remember mumbling to my supervisor that I had to go. I remember praying with my mouth barely open: *Jehovah, please. Please.*

The Move Before the Fall

Even before that call, the energy had shifted. They'd moved Brooke to the heart patient wing—quieter on the surface, colder underneath. One afternoon, a nurse came into our room while I was on the phone with my mother, and started scribbling in a notebook while I talked.

I asked her to step out for privacy. She argued instead. "I can take notes," she snapped.

"For what?" I asked.

She gave no answer.

Two months later—after discharge—I'd find out what those "notes" turned into. Brooke was on oxygen so low I called it a "pinch of breath." I kept asking, "If she doesn't need this, why is it still on? When is she coming home?"

The same shrug of an answer always came: *We're not sure. If you agree to a G-button, maybe two more weeks.*

That G-button had been the drumbeat for months. I'd fought it because Brooke took bottles with me just fine. But I was worn down. They kept saying she'd go home two weeks after the procedure.

I wanted my baby home. I finally said yes.

The day before the coma call, a doctor called: He wanted to "try something different" to help her breathing—nitric oxide. For two hours, it seemed to help. Then he called again: They'd had to call staff in to revive her. She needed to be treated immediately.

The List—Everything and the Kitchen Sink

By the time I reached the NICU after that workday call, the room looked like a medical battlefield. A ventilator loomed over her. IV poles were crowded with bags and lines. At the bedside, the list read:

- Flolan
- Sildenafil
- Precedex
- Morphine

- Sugar through IV
- Saline
- Heparin
- D5
- IV fluids
- Milrinone
- Dexmedetomidine
- Epoprostenol
- Midazolam

I learned later: Flolan increased blood flow so much it caused internal bleeding around her heart. They had to plug a tube into her right side to drain the blood. I can still see the crimson line in that tube—the quiet horror of it—while the machines breathed for her. The NICU smelled like rubbing alcohol mixed with baby powder. A scent I'll never forget.

A nurse touched my arm and spoke in the voice people use when they've already decided for you. "We've done everything we can. We recommend you prepare for the worst."

Later that day, another doctor called and repeated it: "You should prepare for her funeral."

I stared at my untouched sandwich. "If this was your child, would you give up so easily? Jehovah has the final say," I told them. "Not you. Not your charts. Not your prognosis. Jehovah."

I asked them not to come back into my room unless they could speak of life. No more sorrow rehearsals around my baby.

Prayer Shawls and Pep Talks

The chaplain came and handed me a sunshine-colored quilt the nuns had prayed over. "For Brooke," she said.

I draped it across myself while I held my daughter's hand and whispered Isaiah 40:29 under my breath: *He gives power to the tired one...* I was tired enough to dissolve. But that verse held me together.

The lead neonatologist came by, eyes heavy. He said he was sorry and that he would pray. And then there was our primary nurse—the one who'd been with Brooke long enough to love her. She gave her pep talks like coaches give at halftime. "Come on, Brooke. You're sassy. You roll those eyes at us. You are not done here."

My Ritual—The Sound of Home

I made that room a sanctuary. I brought classical CDs. I played R&B—"Miracle" by Whitney Houston and "Silent Prayer" by Shanice and Johnny Gill. I sang until my throat ached. I talked to Brooke about sunshine and fresh sheets and the way our living room looks when morning light slides across the floor.

Skin-to-skin contact became holy ground. I pressed her to my chest so she could map the rhythm of my heart and remember the sound of me breathing. When I had to go to work, my family rotated in. Brooke was never alone.

#Brooketales—The Lifeline

Late at night, when the hospital air turned cold, I wrote. I opened Facebook and poured my heart into #Brooketales. I posted videos of her tiny fingers gripping mine, wrote about the days I was mad, scared, steady. People wrote back—"We're praying." "We're with you." On the worst nights, I scrolled those messages like they were oxygen.

She stayed in that state for three weeks and three days. Every day, one medication came down or came off the list. She began to open her eyes and stare at the IVs and machines, like she was memorizing the enemy. I told her, "You're coming back. I feel you coming back."

The blood drainage slowed, then stopped. The ventilator settings came down. Her oxygen needs dropped. I remember the first time she tried to tug at the tape on her face, stubborn and feisty. There she was—our sassy baby—rolling her eyes at the nurses like she'd always done.

One morning, while I was back at work trying to pretend the world was normal, the hospital number flashed again.

This time, the voice wasn't heavy. "Ms. Hall...she's awake. And she's smiling."

When I reached her room, the machines were still there, but the room felt different—lighter, alive. Brooke's eyes were open, lit from inside. A little smile tugged at the corner of her mouth like she'd been waiting for me to see it.

"You did it," I whispered. "You came back to me."

In that moment, she wasn't just my daughter. She was my champion. The girl who fought the dark and chose light.

Coach's Note

Comas are quiet wars. You don't hear the fighting, but it's happening—inside their little bodies and inside your heart. If you're sitting beside a bed right now, I want you to know: Showing up counts. Your voice counts. Your touch counts. Your prayers count.

Ask questions. Say no when you need to. Demand the why. And when the room feels cold, bring your own warmth—music, scripture, quilts of sunshine.

- **What I needed then:** Permission to say no to funeral preparations and yes to hope, even when medical professionals had given up.
- **What I know now:** Faith isn't denial of medical facts—it's believing in possibilities beyond what science can measure.
- **For the NICU parent reading this:** When they tell you to prepare for the worst, you have every right to prepare for miracles instead. Your baby can hear you fighting for them.

CHAPTER REFLECTIONS

1. What "pep talks" do you need to give yourself right now? Write three sentences you can repeat when fear gets loud.

CHAPTER REFLECTIONS

2. Where did you see small signs of life this week? List them. Small is not the same as insignificant.

CHAPTER REFLECTIONS

3. Who is your "primary nurse" in this season—the voice that keeps cheering when you're tired? Text them a thank-you.

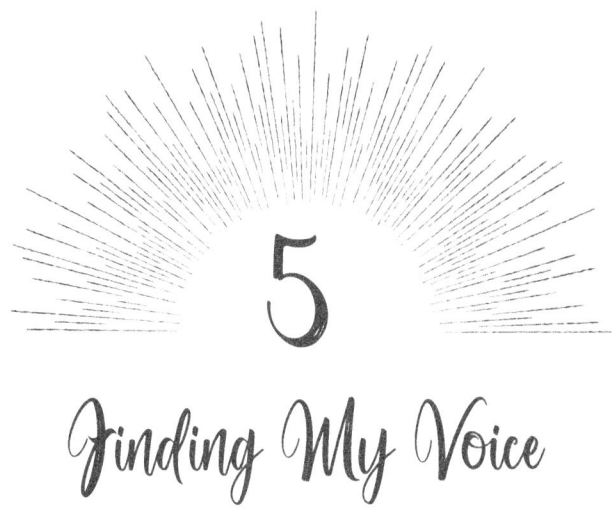

5
Finding My Voice

*"For all things, I have the strength through
the one who gives me power."*
— Philippians 4:13

When Brooke opened her eyes, the room felt different—lighter, like someone had cracked a window in winter and let Purpose blow in. But waking up didn't mean we were home. It meant we were up for the next round.

Medical staff called it a "failure to thrive." I called it a "failure to try."

From the moment Brooke was born, every ounce of her being screamed determination. She was small, yes, but mighty. Yet, the more she grew, the more it felt like the NICU wanted to shrink her progress to fit their timeline.

The Bottle

Brooke loved her bottles. I could tell by the way her tiny fingers curled around the edges. Feeding her was a rhythm only the two of us knew—a heartbeat between us.

But when I wasn't there, something changed. "Oh, I just fed her through the tube," a nurse would casually tell me when I called.

I clenched the phone tighter. "She takes her bottles just fine when I'm there."

"Well, her heart rate went up a little," the nurse would say. To me, it felt like an excuse.

One night, I stayed over. Every alarm that signaled feeding time, I jumped up before a nurse could come. Bottle in hand, I held Brooke close. She drank every ounce, eyes fluttering shut in peace.

The Battle

The battle wasn't just medical. It was emotional. Spiritual. Daily. The NICU is not a place of rest. It's a battlefield dressed up in scrubs and sterile walls.

Every morning, I packed my work bag, then my NICU bag—snacks, water, a blanket for long nights, and, sometimes, a little speaker for music.

The doctors rotated so often that I stopped remembering their names. Instead, I remembered their words. Some were sharp, cutting into my hope. Others were soft, like gauze wrapping around my bleeding faith.

But the script was always the same: "We'll review her file and let you know."

At night, I'd whisper to Brooke, "They don't know you like I do. You're not just a case file. You're mine."

And she'd roll her little eyes at the nurses, as if to say, "Yeah, what Mama said."

Guardian Angels in the NICU

There was a nurse who stuck by Brooke for the entire ten months. She was young, desired to be a mother herself, and became a nurse to advocate for NICU babies. She spoke up for Brooke and me when I had questions that some doctors didn't want to answer.

When Brooke was born, her hair was silky straight. After she grew and developed, it transformed into beautiful, natural curly coils. The nurse often compared that texture to her own red, naturally curly hair to help ease the heavy daily tension. She loved Brooke's determination and cheered for her feisty NICU spirit.

There was a doctor who gave me great advice during his residency. We often talked about Brooke's progress. He was a divorced single father working to save NICU babies, whose special needs son was in the care of home health nurses. One day, I broke down, describing how I didn't know who could assist me after Brooke's release. He looked at me and said home health nurses were my best option and told me not to worry.

I was grateful for the information shared at just the right time.

Beyond the NICU: Instincts at Home

Once Brooke came home, the advocacy didn't stop—it intensified. The hospital sent us home with a formula feeding dosage—the same one she'd received at nine months old. She was now eleven months old, a growing baby. I looked at the measurements, looked at my girl, and knew it wasn't enough.

So I adjusted. Quietly, intentionally. I increased her feeding at night, just slightly. Sure enough, she began to gain weight. At our next doctor's visit, she was no longer underweight.

I brought up my concerns during two appointments. Nothing changed. I finally turned to my home health nurse and said, "Maybe if you tell them, they'll listen to you instead of me."

She did. Suddenly, the doctor changed the formula order. My instincts were right. I was grateful for the nurse's help—but also frustrated. Why hadn't they listened to me?

The Power of Switching Teams

After receiving calls from the hospital caseworker, I knew it was time for a change. I began switching all her doctors in Dallas. I researched the top pediatricians and specialists. I was done being overlooked.

The new team didn't treat me like a sidenote. They were transparent. They broke down the differences between Brooke's health before and after the NICU. They respected me. And most importantly—they saw my daughter.

For the first time in months, I didn't feel dismissed. I felt empowered. They cared not just for Brooke—but for *us*.

More Than Just Brooke

Brooke's journey made me an advocate—not just for her, but for so many others. While she was in her coma, I got certified as a life coach. Something inside me stirred—a knowledge that I was meant to help other women, especially those navigating trauma, rediscover their power and their worth.

If I had to describe my advocacy style in three words: Support. Advance. Represent.

Support is the foundation—I do what I must to ensure fair treatment. Advance is about moving people forward, helping them take steps out of stuckness. Representing means standing in the gap for someone who hasn't yet found their voice.

Coach's Note

Every NICU mom has to learn the language of alarms, diagnoses, and delays. But advocacy? That's a language of the heart. If you're reading this, know that you don't need a medical degree to be your child's voice. You need persistence. You need courage. And most of all, you need faith that what you see in your child is real—even when others dismiss it.

- **What I needed then:** Validation that my observations about Brooke mattered more than rotating doctors' assumptions.
- **What I know now:** Consistency beats expertise when it comes to knowing your child. You see patterns they miss.
- **For the NICU parent reading this:** When you say, "She takes bottles fine with me," that's not a fluke—that's data. Document it. Fight for it. Your child's response to you is medical evidence.

CHAPTER REFLECTIONS

1. When was the first time you truly *trusted your own instincts* over someone else's opinion?

CHAPTER REFLECTIONS

2. How did it feel to be dismissed in a setting where you expected care and clarity?

CHAPTER REFLECTIONS

3. If you had to describe your advocacy style in three words, what would they be?

The Surgeries and Patterns That Made Me Question Everything

"Trust in the LORD with all your heart and lean not on your own understanding; in all your ways submit to Him, and he will make your paths straight."
— Proverbs 3:5-6

I'VE LEARNED THAT IN THE NICU, EVERY SURGERY FEELS LIKE rolling the dice with your child's life. But what I discovered during Brooke's four procedures was that sometimes the most terrifying medical decisions lead to the biggest breakthroughs—and sometimes they lead to more questions than answers.

The First Surgery: PDA Ligation

The doctors explained how premature and full-term babies' hearts develop differently. In some cases, the heart closes naturally after a baby reaches thirty-six weeks. In others, the heart needs surgical intervention to close properly.

Brooke was four months old and making great progress, but she was tiring out during bottle feeding and having issues building stamina. The surgeon counseled me about the effects of PDA surgery and assured me it would help with her sometimes-rapid breathing.

I remember the morning they wheeled her into surgery. My four-month-old baby, already a veteran of countless procedures, looked so small on that gurney. I pressed my hand to the glass as they disappeared through those double doors, whispering the only prayer I could manage: "Jehovah, cover her."

The surgery was completed successfully, but what followed wasn't in any of the pamphlets they'd given me. Another issue developed as her heart healed—she had two ounces of fluid around her heart that were still causing breathing problems.

"We need to place a drainage tube in her left side," the surgeon explained.

I stared at him. "You mean another procedure?"

"It's minor," he said, but nothing feels minor when it's your baby.

That drainage tube became Brooke's companion for two weeks. I watched that line of fluid day and night, praying it would clear. When it finally did, I felt like we'd climbed our first mountain. Brooke was breathing better, taking bottles more easily. For a moment, I thought we were turning the corner.

The Pressure Campaign: The G-Button

The relief didn't last long. Despite Brooke's progress, a new drumbeat started: the G-button procedure. For months, different doctors rotated through, each one suggesting this feeding tube surgery with increasing urgency.

"She needs consistency in her feeding," they said.

"She's not gaining weight fast enough," they added.

"If you want her to come home, this is the path," they concluded.

I fought it. Hard. Brooke took bottles beautifully when I was there.

She loved her pacifier. She didn't have the swallowing issues that typically required a G-button. Every instinct I had screamed that this wasn't necessary.

"Doctor," I said during one particularly frustrating consultation, "she drank every ounce when I fed her last night. Explain to me why she needs surgery."

He avoided my eyes. "Well, her heart rate goes up during feeding."

"Her heart rate goes up when she's excited to see me, too. Are we going to operate on that?"

The nurse beside him shifted uncomfortably. I was asking questions they didn't want to answer.

It felt like a shell game. When I was present, Brooke thrived. When I wasn't, suddenly she couldn't manage what she'd done perfectly just hours before.

The Research Study Papers

One evening, I found paperwork on Brooke's bedside table. Research study information with my name highlighted. The study involved observing premature babies over two months, recording their recovery for research purposes.

When the lead doctor called me about it, I didn't hesitate.

"I choose not to participate," I told her.

The disappointment in her voice was unmistakable. "Are you sure? This could really benefit Brooke's care."

"I'm sure."

I hung up feeling like I'd failed some test I didn't know I was taking. But Brooke wasn't a research opportunity. She was my daughter.

Within weeks of refusing the study, things shifted. New nurses rotated in. Familiar faces disappeared. The doctors who had been warm became clinical. The feeding issues that had seemed manageable suddenly became insurmountable.

The Surgery I Didn't Want

After seven months in the NICU, I was worn down. The daily fights about feeding. The rotating cast of medical professionals who didn't seem to communicate with each other. The constant pressure about the G-button.

"If she gets the G-button, she can go home two weeks after that," the head nurse assured me.

I looked at Brooke, thriving in my arms after finishing another full bottle. She was gaining weight. She was alert and social. But I was tired of fighting the system alone.

"Fine," I said. "Schedule it."

I felt like I was betraying my instincts, but I wanted my baby home more than I wanted to be right.

The G-button surgery went smoothly. Brooke recovered quickly, though she seemed uncomfortable and didn't want anyone touching her belly. Even today, she protects that area when people try to play with her stomach.

I'll admit—feeding and giving medications became easier with the G-button. But what I noticed was that her resistance to taking bottles increased. She'd eat solid foods just fine by mouth, but the bottles became a battle.

We'd taken a step backward in her oral feeding development, not forward.

The Heart Catheterization

The third procedure was a heart catheterization—a diagnostic tool to get a clearer picture of Brooke's heart and lung development. The cardiologist explained that they would send a scope through her lungs and heart to analyze her cardiovascular system in detail.

"In some cases, we can use a type of clamp to open narrow lung passageways and improve oxygen flow," he explained.

Brooke's lungs were small and narrow due to her premature birth. The doctors theorized that her heart had grown in a way that put more pressure on her right ventricle, while the left ventricle wasn't working as hard.

"We hope she'll outgrow this condition," the cardiologist said. "But we want to understand exactly what we're dealing with."

The procedure went well, but the results were puzzling. The condition they'd discovered usually presented at birth, not seven months later. I filed that information away, adding it to my growing list of inconsistencies.

The Diagnosis That Changed Everything

Just when I thought we were making progress, a new diagnosis appeared seemingly overnight: pulmonary hypertension.

After I'd spent two weeks demanding consistent monitoring and challenging the rotating doctors who seemed to know nothing about Brooke's history, I demanded that they do a new echo and swallow study to get facts instead of theories.

"The echo shows pulmonary hypertension," the pulmonologist announced.

I stared at him. "Pulmonary hypertension? She's been here seven months. Every previous echo showed normal results. How does this suddenly appear?"

He couldn't answer that question.

I asked to see the previous echo results. Four normal tests, then suddenly this. The timing felt suspicious—right after I'd refused the research study, right after I'd been challenging their feeding protocols, right after I'd been asking harder questions.

The pieces of a pattern were forming, and I didn't like what I was seeing.

The Growing Suspicion

Looking back, I can see the timeline clearly now. Each time I advocated strongly for Brooke, each time I refused to go along with a recommendation that didn't make sense, the obstacles increased. New diagnoses appeared. Discharge plans got pushed back. Simple procedures became complex.

The research study refusal seemed to be the turning point. After that, I felt like we were no longer fighting Brooke's medical conditions—we were fighting the system itself.

Brooke had been drinking bottles. She had been breathing without an oxygen tube. She had been progressing beautifully. But suddenly, none of that mattered. The goalpost kept moving.

I started keeping my own records. I documented every feeding, every medication, every interaction with staff. If I was going to be treated with suspicion, I was going to arm myself with facts.

Still, Brooke remained in the hospital with very slow progress. Speech and physical therapy came in to help with her development. She was happy some days and fussy others—like any baby. But as she remained hospitalized, I called repeatedly to speak with the doctor on duty about her discharge plan.

After many conversations and adjustments to her feeding expectations, I still couldn't get a clear answer about what milestones she needed to hit to come home. Finally, they'd scheduled the G-button surgery with the promise that she'd be discharged two weeks after.

For the first time in months, we had a concrete plan.

The Calls That Wouldn't Stop

After Brooke's eventual discharge, she didn't return to the emergency room for anything. The home health nurses were surprised and pleased by her progress. But strangely, I continued to get calls from the previous hospital for appointments.

I'd already switched her records completely to a new hospital, yet was experiencing pushback with her Medicare transition. If a child is on Medicare in Texas and lives in Tarrant County, the contract is only with one children's hospital. Since I'd relocated to a borderline area between Dallas and Tarrant County, I hoped Brooke's Medicare could be changed so she could receive care through Dallas Children's Hospital.

I was unsatisfied and frustrated that I was still expected to return somewhere I no longer trust.

The personal questions during these calls had nothing to do with Brooke or my health insurance. They felt like interrogations with uncomfortable, invasive inquiries. I remained as professional as possible, but it got to the point where I was receiving calls for referrals I never made.

I explained to schedulers on multiple occasions that I no longer wanted Brooke to be cared for at their facility. But the calls kept coming.

One thing I've learned: When a hospital can't let go of your case, despite your clear desire to transfer care, there's usually a reason that has nothing to do with your child's medical needs.

The Questions That Remained

The more distance I got from our NICU experience, the clearer the patterns became. Research studies I refused. Feeding progress that was acknowledged when I was present but dismissed when I wasn't. Diagnoses that appeared and disappeared. Procedures that were "essential" until they suddenly weren't.

I don't know if what we experienced was systemic racism, research pressure, financial incentives, or a combination of factors. What I do know is that trusting my instincts—even when it made me seem "difficult"—may have saved my daughter from unnecessary interventions.

The four procedures Brooke underwent taught me that being an advocate means asking hard questions, even when the medical team doesn't want to answer them. It means trusting your own observations of your child, even when experts dismiss them. And it means being willing to fight systems, not just diagnoses.

Sometimes, the most important surgery is the one you refuse to let them perform.

Coach's Note

MEDICAL PROCEDURES ON TINY BODIES FEEL ENORMOUS, but I learned that the hardest part wasn't the surgery itself—it was fighting for transparency about why each procedure was truly necessary. The G-button surgery I fought against ended up being helpful, but my resistance forced important conversations about Brooke's actual needs versus protocol expectations.

- **What I needed then:** Clear explanations of why each procedure was necessary and what the alternatives were if we didn't proceed.
- **What I know now:** The pressure to consent to procedures can increase when you ask too many questions, refuse research participation, or challenge standard protocols. Trust your instincts about your child's capabilities.
- **For the NICU parent reading this:** You have the right to understand every procedure thoroughly, to see all test results, and to get second opinions. When medical teams can't clearly explain why something is necessary, keep asking questions.

CHAPTER REFLECTIONS

1. How do you balance trusting medical expertise with trusting your parental instincts when they conflict?

CHAPTER REFLECTIONS

2. What questions do you wish you had asked before agreeing to procedures or interventions?

CHAPTER REFLECTIONS

3. Have you noticed patterns in how your advocacy style affects the responses you receive from medical staff?

7

The Long Road Home

> *"Be strong and courageous. Do not be afraid;*
> *do not be discouraged, for the LORD your*
> *God will be with you wherever you go."*
> — JOSHUA 1:9

After ten months, the NICU had become our second home. I knew every nurse's schedule, every doctor's bedside manner, every alarm's meaning. The rhythm of that place had synchronized with my heartbeat. So when they finally said the words I'd been desperate to hear—"Brooke can go home"—I felt something I didn't expect: terror.

The Preparation Ritual

The hospital had a strict discharge protocol that felt like boot camp for new parents. Over the course of two weeks, I had to prove I could care for Brooke independently. The list was extensive:

- Watch mandatory videos about "purple crying," crib safety, and emergency infant CPR.
- Complete multiple feeding demonstrations with different nurses.

- Pass a car seat safety test (Brooke had to sit in her seat for ninety minutes without oxygen desaturation.)
- Schedule follow-up appointments with her pediatrician, cardiologist, and pulmonologist.
- Arrange home health nursing and medical equipment delivery.
- Learn to operate her feeding pump, oxygen concentrator, and pulse oximeter.

But the most challenging requirement was the final week: I had to stay at the hospital day and night, providing all of Brooke's care with minimal nursing supervision. This was meant to ease the transition, but it felt like the final test in a course I'd been failing for months.

"You'll essentially be living here," the charge nurse explained. "We need to make sure you're completely comfortable with her care before you take her home."

I nodded, but inside I was screaming. I'd been providing her care for months. I'd been advocating for her when others wouldn't. I'd learned her rhythms better than anyone on staff. Yet I still had to prove myself worthy of taking my own daughter home.

The Emotional Rollercoaster

My coworkers threw me a small party when they heard Brooke was finally coming home. For the first time in months, I felt genuine excitement instead of cautious optimism. My supervisor had been incredibly supportive throughout the entire ordeal, and the team had donated those precious leave hours that allowed me to be present for this final stretch.

"We're so excited for you," my supervisor said, handing me a card signed by the entire office. "You've been through so much."

As I drove to the hospital that afternoon to begin my week-long residency, I felt lighter than I had in months. We were really doing this. Brooke was really coming home.

But the moment I walked into her room with my overnight bag, the weight of what we were leaving behind hit me. This room had been Brooke's entire world. These machines had kept her alive. These nurses had watched her grow from a one-pound micro-preemie to a thriving seven-pound baby.

Some of the staff had become like family. The primary nurse who'd given Brooke pep talks during her darkest days. The respiratory therapist who'd celebrated every decrease in oxygen support. The cleaning lady who always stopped to talk to Brooke and called her "sunshine."

We were leaving our village. And despite everything we'd been through, that felt both liberating and terrifying.

Brooke's Final Week Performance

True to form, Brooke was the star of her own show during discharge week. She was alert, social, and seemed to understand that something important was happening. When familiar faces stopped by her room, she'd light up with her biggest smiles. When strangers tried to handle her, she'd give them her signature eye roll that had earned her the "sassy baby" reputation.

I proceeded with her nightly care routine: diaper changes, feeding, medication administration, temperature checks. I rocked her to sleep while playing her favorite songs—"Miracle" "Silent Prayer." She'd snuggle into my chest and drift off peacefully, just as she had for months.

The first two nights went smoothly. The supervising nurse was patient and kind, offering guidance without hovering. She helped me organize Brooke's complex medication schedule and walked me through operating the feeding pump I'd be taking home.

"You're a natural at this," she said as I efficiently managed Brooke's midnight feeding. "She's lucky to have such a dedicated mother."

For once, I felt seen and appreciated, rather than scrutinized.

The Setback

Midway through the week, Brooke developed congestion. Nothing serious—just the kind of minor cold that would barely slow down a full-term baby. But for a micro-preemie with chronic lung disease, it meant her oxygen needs increased from a quarter-liter to half a liter.

"We'll need to keep her for observation for three more days," the doctor announced.

My heart sank, but I understood. Better safe than sorry. They placed isolation precautions on her room—gowns, gloves, and masks for anyone entering. I felt insulted by the implication that I might have caused her illness, but I told myself it was standard protocol.

During this extended stay, I opened up to one of the nurses about how exhausting the entire journey had been. The constant uncertainty, the rotating cast of medical professionals, the feeling of never knowing what each day would bring.

"It's been such a rollercoaster," I confided. "Some days I feel strong, and other days I feel like I'm barely hanging on."

I didn't know that this conversation would later be documented and twisted into evidence against me. At the time, it felt like a normal human moment—a tired mother finally having someone to talk to.

The Battle Over Basic Needs

By the third day of my hospital residency, I was running on fumes. I'd been wearing the same clothes for 48 hours, had eaten nothing but vending machine snacks, and felt like I needed a shower desperately. When I told the day nurse I was going home briefly to shower and get fresh clothes, her reaction was swift and hostile.

"You cannot leave this hospital for the next 24 hours," she said firmly, then called the charge nurse to repeat the directive.

I stared at them both. "I live fifteen minutes away. I just need to shower and get clean clothes. Would you want to stay somewhere for days without being able to clean up?"

"Those are the rules," the charge nurse said curtly. "If you leave, it could affect Brooke's discharge."

The threat was clear. I felt like I was being treated like a child, or worse—like someone who couldn't be trusted with basic decision-making. Here I was, a federal professional who'd been caring for my daughter for ten months, being told I couldn't step out for basic hygiene.

But I was exhausted and desperate. Despite their warnings, I left to take care of myself.

The Universe's Sense of Humor

As if the situation wasn't stressful enough, my car wouldn't start when I tried to leave the hospital. The battery was completely dead. It took twenty minutes, sitting in the freezing parking garage, for hospital security to come give me a jump start.

When I returned with fresh clothes and food, the nurse's attitude had shifted from hostile to suspicious. She acted like my car trouble was a lie, despite the fact that security could verify the assistance they'd provided.

"Brooke seems fine," she said coldly, even though Brooke was sleeping peacefully.

"Of course she's fine," I replied. "She was sleeping when I left, and she's still sleeping."

But then the nurse did something that revealed her true intentions. "I think she needs her diaper changed," she announced.

I checked Brooke's diaper. Completely dry. When I pointed this out, the nurse walked quickly out of the room and slammed the door.

The message was clear: My brief absence for basic human needs was being treated as abandonment, and any interaction with my daughter would be scrutinized for evidence of my unfitness.

I couldn't believe how petty and vindictive this had become. It was like being punished for being human while caring for my child.

The Angels Among Us

Fortunately, the final day of our hospital stay brought a different nurse—one I recognized from Brooke's early NICU days. He was kind, professional, and genuinely excited about Brooke's homecoming.

"I remember when she was so tiny," he said, gently helping me organize her discharge supplies. "Look at her now! She's amazing."

He walked me through the final discharge instructions, helped me coordinate with the pharmacy about her home medications, and made sure I had all the necessary follow-up appointments scheduled. His warmth and competence reminded me that there were still people in this system who cared about patients and families, not just protocols and power dynamics.

"You've done an incredible job advocating for her," he told me. "Don't let anyone make you doubt that."

His words felt like a blessing after days of feeling criticized and questioned.

The Moment of Truth

Discharge day arrived with surreal clarity. After ten months, two weeks, and three days, we were finally leaving. Brooke had accumulated an impressive collection of belongings during her extended stay: toys from volunteers, clothes in every preemie size, medical equipment, countless paperwork files, and photos documenting her entire journey from micro-preemie to thriving baby.

My uncle came to help transport everything, and we needed every bit of his assistance. My Altima Coupe was completely inadequate for the oxygen tanks, feeding pump, stroller, car seat, and bags of supplies. We loaded items like we were moving houses, which, in a way, we were.

Brooke seemed to understand the significance of the day. She was alert and social, charming every nurse and doctor who stopped in to say goodbye. When I placed her in the car seat for the final time, she looked around with those bright, curious eyes that had captivated everyone from day one.

The walk to the car felt ceremonial. Nurses lined the hallway to wave goodbye. Some had tears in their eyes—the ones who'd genuinely cared for Brooke and celebrated every milestone with us. Others watched with professional courtesy, but little warmth.

As we loaded the car and prepared to drive away, I felt a complex mix of emotions: relief, excitement, gratitude, and an unexpected sadness. This place had been our world for nearly a year. Despite all the challenges and conflicts, it had helped keep my daughter alive and grow strong enough to come home.

The Drive to Freedom

The fifteen-minute drive home felt both eternal and instant. I kept checking the rearview mirror to make sure Brooke was okay, watching for any signs of distress. But she seemed peaceful, occasionally making little cooing sounds as she watched the ceiling of the car.

"We're going home, baby girl," I whispered. "To our own place, with our own things, and our own rules."

For the first time in ten months, no one would wake us up for vitals checks. No alarms would beep all night. No strangers would enter our space without permission. No one would question my decisions about my daughter's care.

As I pulled into my apartment complex and saw my front door, the weight of what we'd accomplished hit me fully. We'd survived the NICU.

We'd outlasted the doubters. We'd proven that Brooke was strong enough, and I was capable enough, to make this work.

The challenges ahead were unknown, but they were ours to face together, as mother and daughter, in the privacy and safety of our own home.

Brooke was finally where she belonged: with me, away from the machines and protocols and constant surveillance that had defined her earliest months. Whatever came next, we'd face it on our own terms.

The long road home was finally behind us. The real journey was just beginning.

Coach's Note

Discharge after a long NICU stay is one of the most complex emotional experiences imaginable. You're desperate to go home, but terrified to leave the safety net that kept your child alive. You're grateful for the care they received, but exhausted by the constant scrutiny of your parenting.

That final testing period felt particularly cruel—being forced to prove my worthiness while dealing with petty power plays from staff who seemed more interested in control than care.

- **What I needed then:** Clear discharge criteria, respect for my basic human needs during the transition week, and acknowledgment that I'd been successfully caring for my daughter for months already.
- **What I know now:** The transition home is as much about psychological preparation as it is about medical readiness. The systems designed to ensure safety can sometimes create additional trauma for families already stretched to their limits.
- **For the NICU parent reading this:** When discharge planning feels like you're being tested rather than supported, trust your instincts about what you and your baby need. The real test isn't whether you can perform care under hospital observation—it's whether you can advocate for your child's wellbeing in any environment.

CHAPTER REFLECTIONS

1. How did you prepare emotionally for taking your child home after an extended hospital stay?

CHAPTER REFLECTIONS

2. What moments during discharge planning made you feel supported versus scrutinized?

CHAPTER REFLECTIONS

3. How do you balance gratitude for medical care with frustration about systemic problems?

CHAPTER REFLECTIONS

4. What would you tell another parent about to begin the discharge process?

8
Life After NICU—The Real Beginning

*"She is clothed with strength and dignity;
she can laugh at the days to come."*
— PROVERBS 31:25

THE SILENCE WAS THE FIRST THING I NOTICED. AFTER TEN months of constant alarms, humming machines, and overhead pages, our apartment felt like a library. Brooke's breathing was the only sound—steady, strong, and beautifully unassisted except for the gentle whisper of oxygen through her nasal cannula.

I stood in the doorway of our living room, holding my daughter in our own space for the first time, and felt something I hadn't experienced in almost a year: peace.

Creating Our Sanctuary

The apartment had been transformed into a medical facility during my preparation for Brooke's homecoming. The living room now housed an oxygen concentrator, feeding pump, pulse oximeter, and enough medical supplies to stock a small clinic. I'd arranged everything with the precision of a NICU nurse—medications organized by time of day, feeding supplies within arm's reach, emergency numbers posted by every phone.

But I'd also made it beautiful. Soft blankets draped over the medical equipment. Family photos on every surface. Fresh flowers on the kitchen table. This wasn't going to be an extension of the hospital—this was going to be our home.

Brooke seemed to sense the difference immediately. As I carried her from room to room, showing her our space, her eyes were wider and more alert than I'd seen them in weeks. No strange faces hovering over her. No unexpected procedures. Just mama's voice and the warm light filtering through our windows.

"This is your room, baby girl," I whispered, settling into the rocking chair I'd placed by her crib. "Your own crib, your own toys, your own little kingdom."

She looked up at me with those bright, curious eyes and made a soft cooing sound that felt like agreement.

The Angels in Scrubs

The home health nursing service became our lifeline in those early weeks. These weren't the rotating cast of hospital staff we'd grown accustomed to—these were professionals who came into our home specifically to help Brooke thrive.

The first nurse who walked through our door was everything I'd hoped for. Experienced, warm, and genuinely excited to meet Brooke after hearing about her NICU journey.

"Oh my goodness, look at you!" she said, immediately charmed by Brooke's alert personality. "You're such a fighter, aren't you?"

She spent the first visit teaching me to operate all the equipment with confidence, but more importantly, she watched how Brooke and I interacted and celebrated what she saw.

"You two have such a beautiful bond," she observed as Brooke settled peacefully in my arms for her feeding. "She knows exactly who her mama is."

After months of having my every move scrutinized and questioned, having a medical professional validate my parenting felt like emotional medicine I didn't know I needed.

The Routine of Freedom

Our days developed a rhythm that felt both structured and liberated. Brooke's medication schedule still governed our mornings and evenings, but the time in between was ours to define. No doctors' rounds interrupting her sleep. No shift changes disrupting our bonding time. No strangers making notes about our interactions.

I'd wake up to her stirring in her crib—not to the harsh sound of an alarm clock or hospital announcement. I'd check her oxygen levels and pulse—but in the soft morning light of our bedroom, not under fluorescent hospital lighting. I'd prepare her feeding—but in my own kitchen, with my own supplies, on my own timeline.

"Good morning, sunshine," I'd whisper as I lifted her from her crib. "Ready for another day in our own place?"

She seemed to understand the difference. Her sleep was deeper and more peaceful. Her appetite was stronger. Her alertness during awake periods was more sustained. It was as if leaving the hospital had unlocked a part of her development that had been suppressed by the institutional environment.

The home health nurses noticed the changes too.

"She's like a different baby," one of them remarked after a week of home visits. "More relaxed, more engaged. Home is definitely where she needed to be."

First Doctor Visits: A New Perspective

Our first pediatric appointment outside the hospital felt monumental. I packed Brooke's portable oxygen, pulse oximeter, and a bag full of medical records, unsure what to expect from a "normal" doctor's office after months of specialist consultations.

The pediatrician was everything the NICU doctors weren't—warm, unhurried, and genuinely impressed by Brooke's progress.

"She looks fantastic," he said, examining her with gentle hands. "Her weight gain is excellent, her muscle tone is strong, and her alertness is remarkable for a baby who's been through what she has."

He asked thoughtful questions about her home routine and seemed genuinely interested in my observations about her development. When I mentioned my concerns about her medication regimen, he didn't dismiss them.

"Let's take a conservative approach," he said. "If she's thriving at home, we don't need to rush any changes, but we also don't need to continue medications that may no longer be necessary."

For the first time in months, I felt like I was being treated as an equal partner in Brooke's care rather than a worried parent who needed to be managed.

The Home Health Nursing Miracle

As the weeks progressed, the nursing staff became like extended family. They celebrated every small milestone with genuine enthusiasm. When Brooke started holding her head up more steadily, they cheered. When she began reaching for toys, they documented it with the excitement of proud aunts.

But more importantly, they advocated for us in ways I hadn't experienced in the hospital. When one of Brooke's medications seemed to be causing some stomach upset, the nurse didn't just note it in her chart—she called the doctor immediately and recommended an adjustment.

"Your mama is right," she told Brooke during one particularly fussy evening. "This medicine isn't making you feel good, is it? Let's get this fixed."

The communication between the nursing staff and Brooke's doctors was seamless and respectful. They presented my observations as valuable medical information rather than emotional concerns to be managed. They treated Brooke as an individual patient with unique needs rather than a case file with standard protocols.

One nurse in particular became special to our journey. She had experience with premature babies and understood the unique challenges of post-NICU adjustment. More importantly, she seemed to genuinely love Brooke.

"She's got such personality," she'd say, laughing as Brooke gave her the signature eye roll that had made her famous in the NICU. "This little girl knows exactly what she wants and isn't afraid to let you know about it."

Discovering Joy in Small Moments

Without the constant stress of hospital protocols and rotating staff, I could finally enjoy being Brooke's mother. Our days were filled with small discoveries that felt like massive victories. The first time she smiled at the sound of my voice from across the room, I cried. The first time she slept through the night without any alarms or oxygen desaturations, I felt like we'd won the lottery. The first time she laughed—a genuine, delighted giggle—I knew we'd turned a corner.

"Did you hear that?" I asked the nurse who was visiting that day. "She laughed!"

"She sure did," the nurse confirmed, beaming. "That's the sound of a happy, healthy baby who feels safe and loved."

These moments of pure joy had been impossible in the hospital environment. There had always been something—an alarm, a procedure, a shift change, a visiting specialist—interrupting our connection. At home, we could exist in these perfect bubbles of mother-daughter bliss without external intervention.

The Equipment Becomes Background

Initially, the medical equipment felt overwhelming. The oxygen concentrator hummed constantly. The pulse oximeter beeped if Brooke moved her foot wrong. The feeding pump required careful calibration and monitoring.

But as the weeks passed, these machines became background noise in our daily symphony. I learned to change oxygen tubing without waking a sleeping baby. I mastered the feeding pump programming while talking on the phone. I could interpret pulse oximeter readings while simultaneously preparing meals.

More importantly, Brooke adapted to the equipment with remarkable grace. She learned to move around with her oxygen tubing without getting tangled. She tolerated her feeding schedule without the resistance she'd shown in the hospital. She seemed to understand that these machines were helping her thrive, not holding her back.

"She's so smart," one of the nurses observed. "Look how she's learned to work with her equipment instead of fighting it. That's going to serve her well as she continues to grow."

Early Signs of Thriving

By the end of our first month home, the changes in Brooke were undeniable. Her weight gain accelerated beyond hospital projections. Her sleep patterns became more regular and restful. Her awake periods were longer and more engaged.

Most remarkably, her personality began to shine in ways the hospital environment had never allowed. She was naturally social, lighting up when visitors came over. She was curious about everything, turning her head toward new sounds and studying new faces with intense concentration. She was strong-willed, making her preferences known with increasingly sophisticated communication.

She's not just surviving anymore, I realized during a particularly sweet evening routine. She's actually living.

The contrast with our hospital experience was stark. In the NICU, every day had been about managing crises and meeting minimum standards. At home, every day was about discovering new capabilities and celebrating growth.

The Physical Transformation

The visual changes in Brooke were remarkable. Her skin, which had always been pale and sometimes translucent, developed a healthy pink glow. Her hair, which had been fine and sparse, began growing in thicker and showing off her natural curls. Her muscles, which had been weak from months of limited mobility, strengthened rapidly as she had more freedom to move and stretch.

But the most noticeable change was in her eyes. The alertness and curiosity had always been there, but now there was something else—contentment. She looked like a baby who felt secure and loved, not like a patient enduring treatment.

"Look at those cheeks!" visitors would exclaim. "She looks like a completely different baby!"

The weight gain was impressive, but it was the quality of her development that truly amazed everyone who saw her. This wasn't just a baby getting bigger—this was a baby blossoming into her full potential.

Building Our Support Network

While the hospital had provided medical expertise, our home environment allowed us to build a support network based on genuine care and understanding. The home health nurses became advocates and friends. Our pediatrician became a trusted advisor who respected my insights about Brooke's needs.

But beyond the medical team, we began connecting with our community in ways that hadn't been possible during the hospital months. Neighbors stopped by to meet the baby they'd heard so much about. Coworkers visited to see how we were adjusting. Family members could finally hold Brooke in a relaxed environment without the intimidation of hospital protocols.

"She's so much more relaxed here," my mother observed during her first extended visit to our apartment. "You both are. This is where you were meant to be."

The Turning Point

About six weeks after discharge, I had a moment of clarity that felt like emerging from a tunnel into sunlight. I was feeding Brooke her evening bottle, watching her content face in the soft lamp light, listening to the gentle hum of her oxygen concentrator, and I realized something profound:

We weren't NICU patients anymore. We weren't medical cases being managed. We weren't problems to be solved.

We were simply a mother and daughter, living our lives, growing stronger together in the safety and love of our own home.

The fear that had dominated every day for almost a year began to lift. Not completely—I was still vigilant about her medical needs and careful about her care—but the constant anxiety about survival gave way to excitement about the future.

"We made it, baby girl," I whispered as she drifted off in my arms. "We really made it."

For the first time since her premature birth, I allowed myself to dream about what was coming next instead of just surviving what was happening now. Dance classes. Birthday parties. First words. First steps. Ordinary moments that would be extraordinary because we'd fought so hard to reach them.

The Real Beginning

Looking back, I realize that bringing Brooke home wasn't only the end of our NICU journey—it was the beginning of our real life together. The hospital had been about keeping her alive and getting her strong enough to leave. Home was where we discovered who she really was and who we were going to become together.

The medical equipment would eventually disappear. The nursing visits would decrease and then stop. The appointments would become routine rather than crisis management. But the foundation we built in those first months at home—the trust, the joy, the pure love of being together without institutional interference—that would last forever.

Every evening, as I tucked Brooke into her own crib, in her own room, surrounded by her own things, I felt grateful not just for her survival, but for the privilege of watching her bloom into the remarkable little person she was always meant to be.

The real journey was just beginning, and it was going to be beautiful.

Coach's Note

The transition from hospital to home revealed just how much the institutional environment had been limiting both Brooke's development and our bonding. In our own space, with supportive home health care, she flourished in ways that months of hospital care hadn't achieved. This taught me that sometimes the best medicine isn't medical at all—it's the safety, love, and freedom to develop naturally.

- **What I needed then:** Confidence that I could manage her medical needs at home, and validation that the changes I was seeing were real progress, not just wishful thinking.
- **What I know now:** The environment shapes healing as much as medical intervention. Being home provided the emotional and psychological conditions for Brooke to thrive in ways the hospital never could.
- **For the NICU parent reading this:** When you finally get home, allow yourself to feel the relief and joy. Trust that your child may bloom in ways you haven't seen before. The medical support is important, but your love and the peace of home are medicine too.

CHAPTER REFLECTIONS

1. How did your home environment differ from the hospital in supporting your child's development?

CHAPTER REFLECTIONS

2. What surprised you most about your child's adjustment to being home?

CHAPTER REFLECTIONS

3. How did having medical support in your own space change the dynamic of care?

CHAPTER REFLECTIONS

4. What moments made you realize you'd truly transitioned from survival mode to living mode?

9
The Cost of Fighting and the System's Response

"And my God will meet all your needs according to the riches of His glory in Christ Jesus."
— PHILIPPIANS 4:19

"Do not be afraid, for I am with you. Do not be anxious, for I am your God."
— ISAIAH 41:10

THEY NEVER TELL YOU THAT FIGHTING FOR YOUR CHILD'S LIFE will cost you more than the medical bills. They don't mention that the system designed to help families like yours will become another battle you have to wage while your baby is still learning to breathe.

The Financial Maze

The NICU bills started arriving while Brooke was still hospitalized. Each envelope felt like a small bomb in my mailbox. Even with insurance, the numbers were staggering. But it wasn't just the big-ticket items that drained my accounts—it was the daily necessities that added up, like water filling a leaky boat.

Formula alone was forty-four dollars per can, and Brooke consumed at least one and a half cans every two days. I did the math: more than six-hundred dollars a month just for formula. Then there were the medical supplies that insurance didn't cover, the gas for daily hospital visits, the parking fees that accumulated into hundreds of dollars, and the meals I grabbed between work and NICU shifts because I was too exhausted to cook.

Medical equipment filled my apartment after discharge. Oxygen tanks, nasal cannula machines, a compressor that hummed constantly—each piece representing both hope and financial strain. The home health service delivered supplies monthly, but coordinating with insurance, Medicare, and the equipment company felt like a full-time job I didn't have time for.

The Bureaucratic Marathon

My first visit to the Social Security Administration felt like entering a maze designed to exhaust people into giving up. I took time off work, arriving at eight o'clock in the morning with a folder full of documentation, only to wait in a line that snaked around the building.

"Next window," the clerk called after three hours.

I explained Brooke's situation—micro-preemie, low birth weight, extended NICU stay. According to the social worker at the hospital, she qualified automatically for benefits.

"We'll process this and call you," the representative said, barely looking at my paperwork.

Brooke was approved for the minimum benefit: thirty dollars a month. Thirty dollars. I spent more than that on gas driving to their office.

Six months later, I had to return for a review. Another marathon day, another line that tested my patience and sanity. This time, the representative had different news.

"Due to your income, Brooke no longer qualifies for benefits."

I stared at him. "She's medically declared disabled. How does my income change her medical condition?"

"It's about household size and income limits. You make too much to qualify."

"Too much?" I wanted to laugh, but nothing was funny. "I'm a single mother with medical bills that exceed my rent."

He shrugged. "You could submit paperwork proving you make less money than reported."

The suggestion felt insulting. I was supposed to lie about my income to get help for my disabled daughter? I was being punished for working, for maintaining my career through the hardest year of my life.

I felt outraged, discouraged, and discriminated against—a single, middle-income mother caught in a gap between "too poor" and "rich enough." I made too much for assistance, but not enough to absorb the crushing costs of Brooke's care.

The WIC Office Runaround

My experience with Health and Human Services wasn't much better. The first month of Brooke's life, they provided fruits, vegetables, juice, and eggs. I was grateful for any help.

After her discharge, I returned to update her paperwork, hoping for continued support. The caseworker reviewed my information with the enthusiasm of someone processing parking tickets.

"You qualify for one can of formula per month."

One can. When Brooke needed fifteen cans monthly. The time I spent sitting in that office, filling out forms, and navigating their system was worth more than the single can they offered.

I thanked them, but realized this wasn't help—it was theater. A system designed to look like support while providing just enough assistance to say they tried.

The Hidden Costs

What the financial counselors never mention are the hidden costs of NICU advocacy. The income I lost taking unpaid leave for appointments and emergencies. The career advancement opportunities I missed because I couldn't travel or work overtime. The mental health toll that affected every aspect of my productivity.

I was earning a decent federal salary, but between medical expenses, childcare for doctor visits, and the constant financial pressure, I felt like I was drowning in slow motion. I was too successful to qualify for help, but not successful enough to handle everything alone.

Every month brought new bills, new insurance denials, new prior authorization battles. I spent hours on hold with pharmaceutical companies, fighting for medication approvals. The appeals process for denied claims became a second job I performed in the margins of my actual work.

The irony wasn't lost on me: I was fighting insurance companies by day and advocacy battles by night, all while being labeled "difficult" for asking questions about my daughter's care.

The Knock That Shattered Peace

Two days after bringing Brooke home, I was finally breathing. The apartment was baby-proofed, supplies were organized, and for the first time in ten months, my daughter was sleeping in her own crib instead of a hospital bed.

Three knocks on the door shattered that peace.

"Who is it?" I called, holding Brooke.

"Child Protective Services. Are you Ms. Hall?"

The words hit like ice water. I opened the door to find a woman with a clipboard and an expression that suggested she'd rather be anywhere else.

"I'm here about a complaint from the hospital," she said. "There are allegations that you may be an unfit mother, with recommendations that Brooke be removed from your home."

My heart sank, but I wasn't shocked. I was angry, insulted—but not surprised. The pattern of retaliation had started in the NICU. Now it was following us home.

The Report That Tried to Define Me

She read from her notes: "Staff submitted reports alleging emotional unavailability, statements about abandoning the child at the hospital, failure to connect with the baby, and inability to handle special needs."

Each accusation felt like a slap. Emotional unavailability? I'd spent ten months living between the NICU and my apartment, fighting for my daughter's life. Abandoning her? I'd been there more than some of the staff.

"These allegations seem exaggerated," the caseworker admitted. "I'm closing this case today."

She paused, looking uncomfortable. "Honestly, I was disturbed by the volume of notes taken during your hospital visits. It's like someone was trying to build a case."

There it was—confirmation of what I'd suspected. My advocacy hadn't just been unwelcome; it had been weaponized against me.

The Pattern Becomes Clear

Looking back, I can see the timeline clearly. Every time I questioned a diagnosis, challenged a procedure, or refused to comply with recommendations I found questionable, the pressure increased. My questions weren't being heard as a mother's legitimate concerns—they were being documented as evidence of my unfitness.

The research study I refused. The G-button I initially resisted. The discharge delays I challenged. Each advocacy moment had been twisted into ammunition for a narrative I never knew was being written.

I thought about all those strange interactions—nurses taking notes during personal phone calls, asking invasive questions unrelated to Brooke's care, the sudden shift in staff attitudes after I started pushing back against protocols.

They hadn't just been treating my daughter; they'd been studying me. And when I didn't perform motherhood the way they expected—quiet, compliant, grateful—I became a problem to be solved.

The Emotional Tax

The financial strain was crushing, but the emotional toll was worse. Every bill reminded me that advocating for Brooke came with a price tag. Every denied claim felt like punishment for asking questions. Every bureaucratic hurdle seemed designed to exhaust me into submission.

I was grieving the motherhood experience I'd imagined, while simultaneously fighting systems that seemed determined to prove I wasn't worthy of the one I had. I was too loud, too questioning, too involved. But when I stepped back, I wasn't involved enough.

The CPS visit crystallized something I'd been feeling but couldn't name: The system wasn't just failing to support us—it was actively working against us. Not because Brooke wasn't getting good care, but because I refused to accept inadequate care quietly.

The Cost of Being Right

Research shows that NICU mothers are at a significantly higher risk of developing postpartum depression. The financial stress, medical trauma, and systemic challenges create perfect storm conditions for mental health crises. When you add retaliation for advocacy to that mix, the psychological burden becomes almost unbearable.

I was running on fumes—emotionally, financially, and physically. My self-care had evaporated. I was living on adrenaline and prayer, fighting battles I never should have had to fight while caring for a medically complex baby.

But here's what they didn't count on: Every attempt to silence me only strengthened my resolve. Every bureaucratic obstacle only sharpened my advocacy skills. Every accusation only clarified my purpose.

The True Support System

While government systems failed us and medical institutions targeted us, real support came from unexpected places. Coworkers donated 310 hours of leave time so I could be home with Brooke. Friends brought meals and listened to me vent. Family members drove hours to help with appointments.

My Facebook community rallied around #Brooketales, offering prayers, encouragement, and practical advice. Women I'd never met shared their own NICU stories and survival strategies. This grassroots network understood what the official systems couldn't—that supporting NICU families means more than providing minimal benefits and monitoring compliance.

The home health nursing service became a lifeline, not just for medical care but for emotional support. These nurses had seen other families navigate similar challenges. They knew which battles to fight and which systems to work around.

Finding Our Footing

Despite the financial strain and systemic hostility, Brooke and I found our rhythm. I learned to navigate insurance appeals like a paralegal. I discovered which assistance programs were worth the paperwork and which were designed to discourage applicants.

Most importantly, I learned that being labeled "difficult" by systems that profit from compliance isn't an insult—it's a badge of honor. My questions saved Brooke from unnecessary procedures. My persistence prevented dangerous medication errors. My "difficult" advocacy probably saved her life.

The bills kept coming, and the bureaucratic battles continued, but I stopped expecting fairness from systems designed to benefit institutions over individuals. Instead, I focused on building the support network we actually needed.

The Lesson in the Ledger

Looking at the financial records from that first year, the numbers tell a story of a system that claims to support disabled children while creating insurmountable barriers for their families. But between the lines of those receipts and denied claims is another story—of a mother who learned that the most expensive thing in NICU life isn't the medical bills.

It's the cost of refusing to be silent.

The price of asking questions they don't want to answer.

The toll of fighting systems that punish advocacy.

But also the value of discovering that your voice—however inconvenient to others—is your child's most powerful medicine.

Coach's Note

The financial and emotional costs of NICU advocacy aren't talked about enough. You're fighting for your child's life while systems designed to help instead create additional barriers. The irony of being "too successful" for help while drowning in medical costs reveals how these programs often fail the families who need them most.

- **What I needed then:** Clear information about all available resources and realistic expectations about what I'd actually qualify for, plus protection from retaliation for asking hard questions.
- **What I know now:** The bureaucracy is designed to exhaust you into giving up. Document everything, build your own support network, and know that being "difficult" often means being an effective advocate.
- **For the NICU parent reading this:** Start financial paperwork early, keep detailed records of all expenses, and don't take the first "no" as final. Your advocacy is not a character flaw—it's your job as a parent.

CHAPTER REFLECTIONS

1. What financial surprises have you encountered that no one warned you about?

CHAPTER REFLECTIONS

2. How do you balance fighting for benefits with protecting your time and energy?

CHAPTER REFLECTIONS

3. When have you been made to feel like advocacy was being used against you?

CHAPTER REFLECTIONS

4. What support systems have been most helpful in managing both financial and emotional costs?

KRISTEE HALL

Watching Her Bloom

"I can do all things through Christ who strengthens me."
— Philippians 4:13

The first year was self-defining for Brooke. She continued to blossom with a big personality. She started walking almost immediately after coming home, saying catchphrases like "Oh yeah." She took off in her walker like a jet, and loved listening to "Happy" by Pharrell. That was her favorite song—she would start dancing and smiling, stepping closer to the TV to watch the video.

When the home health nurses came over, she was excited to have extra protection. They were a saving grace; I went to work knowing she was in safe hands. Her favorite shows were Baby Einstein, Bubble Guppies, Super Why, and Cocomelon. Every evening, her fascination with colors and sounds became our quiet celebration—our shared reminder that the world was safe again.

A Mother's Mission

At her doctors' visits, I watched her transform from a small, fragile baby into a solid and sturdy girl, ready to take on anything. My first mission was to get her off the twenty medications she was still taking—the last memory of the NICU that I wanted gone. Each pill represented a reminder of ten months spent tethered to alarms.

After each visit, I asked the doctors, "How much longer would she need these medications?" Most were used by adults with serious health issues. I was leery of Brooke becoming dependent. I went into "plan, execution, and stealth mode," projecting to have her off medications within a month after release.

But something strange started happening. When I wrote her visits in the nurse's journals, a substitute nurse was sent on doctor visit days.

One day, there seemed to be an emotional rush. The doctor kept asking the nurse if I was using the prescribed oxygen in the house. In a raised voice, he said, "Did you see the oxygen being used in the house?" The nurse looked terrified. "No—I did not see oxygen." This nurse knew nothing about us. That ended up being her first and last visit.

Once I noticed this pattern, I inquired into other home health services. That's when I found a minority-owned provider, a former NICU nurse who started her business to advocate for fragile babies. She stepped in and became like family. She was the nurse who helped Brooke with her first steps. She helped me move when I became a homeowner in Texas.

New Beginnings, New Battles

About two months after NICU release, I bought my first home in Texas—in a beautiful neighborhood close to the Cowboys Stadium in Arlington. The move went smoothly. It was a milestone because I officially transferred Brooke's doctor visits to a Dallas children's hospital.

During Brooke's first month at the new hospital, the doctor told me he spoke with previous physicians about her condition. When he evaluated her, he seemed to be in disbelief. "How was she able to recover so fast?" He said the notes "just didn't add up" to the healthy, thriving girl in front of him.

Our first meeting was lukewarm, but we grew close. Brooke enjoyed those bright, wide halls. She excelled in her follow-ups and, one day, suddenly all twenty medications were gone! With prayer and persistence, Brooke was finally medication-free!

We celebrated when I took her to the hospital to remove the G-button. The day we walked in, the receptionist said, "Ms. Hall, you need to speak with our nurse in private about your new home details before moving forward." I answered their questions, paid the $150 co-pay after surgery, and left. I vowed never to set foot in that hospital again.

Brooke began eating even more. She was always open to trying new foods. One evening, a nurse laughed as she told me, "Oh, Brooke painted today." I laughed back. "She doesn't know how to paint yet." The nurse smiled. "No, I put peas on her tray, and she splattered them all over my scrubs." Green lines marked the fabric like abstract art. That day, we decided peas were off the table (and to this day, she still hates them).

Strengthened by the Storm

My first year of motherhood is hard to describe. I didn't have a moment to process it, but I became tuned in to my daughter instantly. I became a caregiver, advocate, nurturer, and mother bear. I wanted to protect my cub as fiercely as I could. I already felt guilty for Brooke's early birth and knew I had to ensure she was okay every single day.

There is no other explanation for how we went from survival mode to thriving mode—except faith. I knew we'd make it, no matter what obstacles. I matured so much as a woman. Motherhood was becoming on me, and I cherished each moment! I was no longer just a single professional woman—I was bound in purpose to a daughter who depended on me. Motherhood crystallized my strength into an urgent, divine mission: to protect Brooke at all costs.

Coach's Note

This chapter is where survival begins to give way to life—where medical charts give way to personality, and independence blooms in a once-fragile child. Recognize that nourishing a baby's body can also ignite your own transformation. Motherhood wasn't what happened to me—it revealed the real me.

- **What I needed then:** Evidence that all the fighting, the sleepless nights, and the advocacy would actually lead to something beautiful.
- **What I know now:** Every milestone your child hits is also your milestone. Their growth is proof of your fierce love in action.
- **For the NICU parent reading this:** When your baby takes their first independent breath, walks their first step, says their first word—celebrate yourself too. You fought for those moments.

CHAPTER REFLECTIONS

1. Think back to a moment when your child showed a spark of independence. How did that make you feel?

CHAPTER REFLECTIONS

2. Were there systems that felt like barriers after you left the hospital? How did you navigate them?

CHAPTER REFLECTIONS

3. What personal growth came from your journey—not just for your child, but for you?

The Freedom We Fought For

> *"So do not throw away your confidence; it will be richly rewarded. You need to persevere so that when you have done the will of God, you will receive what He has promised."*
> — Hebrews 10:35-36 (NIV)

The hardest part was over now. The medications were finally gone. I was so relieved that my daughter was no longer the guinea pig! The moment they stopped, I threw away all documentation that reminded me of that time. With one firm tug, the medical files, dosage schedules, and printed prescription labels hit the trash, and I exhaled a breath I didn't realize I had been holding for ten long months.

Clearing the Shelf

This was the first of many expected reliefs. No more monitoring doses. No more post-visits confirming how each dose was working. The home health care nurses and I stayed up tirelessly after Brooke was asleep, going over each medication and dosage. We sat on the floor in dim light, flipping through records like detectives, our whispers laced with concern and conviction.

My faith and instincts guided us as she overcame each week during the elimination process. The oxygen was first to go—it always seemed like a joke. Even family and friends would laugh at the dosage level and say, "Only because you have good insurance." I asked the doctor on the last visit for official permission to remove her from meds, and the request was granted. Finally, Brooke was breathing independently—free from oxygen, free from pills, free from medical dependence.

The Silver Lining

For some reason, I trusted these new doctors immediately. They gave us respect and were transparent with their medical advice. They showed us care and consideration. When asked a question, they gave clear and correct answers. Their language was plain, their tone warm. I was finally being seen and heard after ten months of feeling like a ghost mother.

I am forever grateful for the experience of having the best doctors at such a delicate time. They were heaven-sent. Finally, I felt the burdens lifted off my shoulders. Not only were these the correct physicians, but they also came highly recommended from the owner of the home healthcare service, who had a long professional relationship with these physicians.

On doctor visits, Brooke enjoyed the receptionist and office staff. She liked running down the hallways and playing with toys. The drive was scenic as we drove the George Bush Parkway into Dallas's medical district. I looked forward to visits. The doctors were gentle and kind. Each visit showed a stamp of approval and great health. Doctors asked about Brooke's previous NICU stay and were amazed at her story. "You should write about this," they said. I smiled, not knowing I actually would one day.

She continued to thrive. After getting off medications, the visits slowed down and then stopped altogether. As we neared her first birthday, the home health care services would stop soon, and Brooke would need a new caregiver.

A New Routine, A New Rhythm

Her name was Queenie. She came highly recommended by a nurse. At first, she was reluctant on the phone. Then we finally spoke in person. She had previous experience with preemie NICU kiddos and even had one of her own who was preemie. The minute I told her about Brooke's NICU experiences, she was on board.

She was amazed at how small Brooke was—to have survived the NICU so valiantly! When we visited her home, she had everything we needed. A small garden house, a kids' slide, a computer area, and a patio. Four furry babies—two chihuahuas and two miniature schnauzers—roamed freely as lively mascots for the daycare. It was a world of color and chaos and calm.

She had a great spirit and became instantly attached to Brooke. She was an excellent cook and introduced Brooke to soul food, Mexican, and wholesome dishes. The kids at daycare became Brooke's new best friends. Queenie's kids also became attached to Brooke—her son was an aspiring firefighter, and her daughter had beautiful red curls larger than life. The house was always full of people, pets, and joy.

Thriving Among Friends

On some weeks when I traveled, Queenie kept Brooke overnight. I was blessed to have met this family. One of Brooke's daycare buddies was her partner in mischief. He was a big, cute kid, and Brooke was the small but fiery girl. They often played together, made messes, and cried when one left before the other.

Then there were two more—a girl and a boy—both younger but so busy. Brooke treated them as her little brother and sister. She showed them how to count and often tried to boss them around. Once the girl got bigger, she started bossing Brooke around. That's when I knew—my little cub was learning to thrive among the pack.

I was thankful for how fast Brooke was socializing with kids and learning to play with puppies. The chihuahuas often ran outside and came back to the door themselves. It was lively and such a great environment for my thriving girl.

Coach's Note

MY TRANSITION FROM MEDICALLY-DEPENDENT SURVIVAL TO holistic thriving was not just physical—it was deeply spiritual. The removal of Brooke's medications marked the beginning of a deeper transformation. Trust became the new currency—trust in my daughter's strength, trust in medical care finally aligned with my instincts, and trust in the universe to send the right people to us.

Caregivers like Queenie didn't just show up by accident; they were answered prayers that reminded me I wasn't alone. The same mother who once questioned whether her voice mattered in the NICU now had a network of support built on her determination to advocate for her child.

- **What I needed then:** Proof that saying no to unnecessary medical interventions was the right choice for my child.
- **What I know now:** Freedom from the medical system's control feels like breathing again. Trust your instincts about what your child truly needs.
- **For the NICU parent reading this:** When doctors can't explain why medications are still needed despite improvement, keep questioning. Your child's wellness is not their research opportunity.

CHAPTER REFLECTIONS

1. How does it feel when the burden finally begins to lift?

CHAPTER REFLECTIONS

2. Who were the "Queenie figures" in your life who stepped in when you needed them?

CHAPTER REFLECTIONS

3. In what ways did you reclaim your power after a period of helplessness?

12
Home Sweet Victory

"She opens her mouth with wisdom, and the teaching of kindness is on her tongue."
— Proverbs 31:26

The victory wasn't just in survival—it was in the way Brooke claimed her space in the world with the confidence of someone who had fought for every breath and won. Watching her grow from a one-pound micro-preemie into a thriving toddler felt like witnessing a daily miracle, but it was the *quality* of her development that took my breath away.

Blossoming Into Her Own

My most rewarding moments as a mother became seeing Brooke grow and evolve every day, especially knowing she was proving wrong every naysayer from our NICU journey. As a natural competitor, I reveled in the moments when Brooke set each new milestone. Her first steps, words, and play dates weren't just developmental markers—they were victory laps around every prediction that had tried to limit her future.

After moving to our new townhome in Arlington, the fresh beginning set a tone of comfort that both Brooke and I felt the moment we walked through those doors. This wasn't just a change of address—it was a declaration of independence from the medical world that had defined our first year together.

The new space became Brooke's playground in ways the apartment never could. She would climb into her walker and speed away across the kitchen floor like she was making up for lost time. I found myself running behind her just to keep up, marveling at this tiny tornado who had once been tethered to machines.

When my mother came to visit, she laughed and said, "I've never seen a baby run in a walker before." But I saw it differently—this was Brooke's declaration that she was done being careful, done being fragile, done being the baby everyone worried about.

The Art of First Steps

Brooke's first independent steps came not from cautious encouragement, but from pure determination and a touch of sibling rivalry with her toys. Her home health nurse had become like family, understanding Brooke's stubborn streak better than most.

"Watch this," the nurse said one afternoon, taking one of Brooke's favorite toys up the stairs. "I'm going to see if Brooke will follow."

Brooke had grown cautious about walking after a scary fall in the kitchen weeks earlier. She'd crawl at lightning speed but hesitate when we tried to get her to walk. But that day, watching her beloved toy disappear up the stairs, something shifted.

"Come on, Brooke," the nurse called from halfway up. "If you want this toy, you have to come get it."

I watched my daughter pause at the bottom of the stairs, processing this challenge with the seriousness of a chess master. She looked at the toy, looked at the stairs, looked back at me as if to say, "Are you seeing this nonsense?"

Then she started climbing.

Not crawling—climbing. One determined step after another, pausing at each level to survey her kingdom below before continuing her ascent. When she reached the toy, we expected her to sit down and play. Instead, she stood up, took five deliberate steps toward us, and smiled like she'd just conquered Mount Everest.

"Look at our Brookie!" We cheered. "She's arrived!"

In that moment, I silently told every doctor who had questioned her mobility to eat their words. Brooke hadn't just learned to walk—she'd chosen her moment to shine.

Words of Wonder

I never doubted that words would come early and often for Brooke. Even in the NICU, Brooke had been a chatterbox. She would look at me and launch into elaborate baby conversations that felt like she was sharing state secrets. When I showed my mother videos of these one-sided discussions, she laughed and said, "We have a mouthy one."

We were watching television one evening when I placed her in her high chair for dinner. Out of nowhere, she started saying, "Oh yeah!" with the enthusiasm of a game show contestant.

"Brooke, where did you get this phrase from?" I asked, trying not to laugh.

"Oh yeah!" she repeated, then twice more for emphasis.

Not only was she chatty—she was funny. Her comedic timing was already impeccable.

When my mother visited, Brooke started calling her "Nana" without any prompting from us. She called me "Momma" when she cried, and saved her random vocabulary surprises for the strangest moments. The chatter never stopped, as if she'd been saving up conversations during those ten months of medical silence.

Her words came as fast as she moved in her walker—a rapid-fire stream of consciousness that filled our home with the sound of pure joy.

Little Community Explorer

Brooke's first real social adventure came during a play date with my nurse's son at the mall in Grapevine. As I pushed both children in a double stroller, watching them laugh at each other and gesture wildly, I realized this was the childhood I had dreamed of during those long NICU nights.

When we released them to run around the mall's play area, I felt my heart catch in my throat. Brooke was still getting steady on her legs, and I worried about her falling with so many strangers watching.

"Relax," the nurse said, reading my anxiety. "They're kids. They need to get their energy out so they can crash later."

She was right. I took a deep breath and watched my daughter make friends with the fearless confidence of someone who had never been told she was different. She and the little boy got along beautifully, and when it was time to leave, both children cried like their hearts were breaking.

This became our pattern—Brooke gravitating toward other children with magnetic enthusiasm. She would spot a toddler across a room and light up, ready to introduce herself with a big "Brooke!" and an expectant smile.

Sometimes I'd catch myself saying, "Girl, these kids don't want to play with you," when other children seemed standoffish. But Brooke never took rejection personally. She'd simply move on to the next potential friend with unshakeable optimism.

At daycare with Queenie, this social butterfly tendency reached full bloom. Brooke took younger children under her wing, turned playtime into elaborate productions, and somehow convinced other kids to participate in her increasingly creative mischief.

"You will not believe what Brookie and her protégés did today," Queenie would report at pickup, shaking her head with fond exasperation.

"Oh no, what now?" became my standard response.

They were hiding toys behind bookshelves, sneaking outside to the slide, and generally treating daycare like their personal kingdom. I had conversations with Brooke about sharing and kindness, but secretly, I loved her leadership skills.

Home Is Where Hope Lives

No matter how busy or challenging my workday became, I lived for the moment when I'd turn my key in the door and see Brooke's face light up. The ritual of picking her up and walking through each room of our house—showing her the clothes in her closet, the toys in her basket, the photos on our walls—became my daily reminder that we had built something beautiful together.

I'll admit, as a new mother to a baby girl, I developed a small shopping habit that needed managing. Brooke had name-brand shoes, adorable jackets, dress sets, and enough toys to stock a small boutique. Shopping for her became my therapy—every outfit a celebration of the future I'd once feared we might not have.

After the first year, I had to slow down. She grew out of clothes so fast that I was essentially donating brand-new items monthly. But those early shopping sprees weren't really about the clothes—they were about hope made tangible.

The Contrast: Hospital vs. Home

The difference between our NICU experience and home life was like comparing black-and-white photography to full color. In the hospital, I had felt like I was suiting up for battle every day—helmet, gloves, and protective armor—against a system that seemed designed to break us down.

Every milestone in the NICU had felt like a negotiation rather than a celebration. The environment kept us boxed in, always waiting for permission to hope, always bracing for the next setback or delay. The NICU brought constant alarms, revolving medical staff, and an undercurrent of paranoia about what negative assessment might be lurking in the next shift report. The hospital had felt cold, institutional, designed to remind us daily that we were patients rather than people. One nurse had even told me Brooke would "walk crooked and have brain issues."

The casual cruelty of that prediction still makes my blood boil. What kind of person says that to a mother about her child?

At home, each milestone became an adventure. Brooke's nurses gave me insights I could trust, listened to my concerns without judgment, and addressed issues with her doctors as partners rather than gatekeepers. Our home brought positive energy that I controlled. I was comfortable, confident, and at ease. Instead of fear and defensiveness, I felt hope and possibility. Home was where safety, stability, and heart lived—undeniably and abundantly.

Both Brooke and I blossomed once we escaped that institutional environment. She developed her personality without medical interpretation, and I rediscovered my maternal instincts without constant second-guessing.

The Doctor Who Changed Everything

Our post-NICU medical experiences were a revelation. The most transformative visit was our final appointment with the cardiologist who had guided us through Brooke's heart journey.

This doctor had become one of my favorites, and I felt genuine sadness knowing we would no longer need his expertise. Brooke shared my affection—she would literally race to his office when the elevator doors opened, like she was visiting a beloved uncle.

During that final visit, he checked her height, weight, and heart function with the thoroughness that had always characterized his care. Then he did something that moved me to tears.

"Ms. Hall," he said, "I want to commend you for being such an outstanding advocate for Brooke. Don't ever stop speaking up for her the way you do."

His words felt like absolution after months of being labeled "difficult" for asking questions and demanding answers. This doctor understood that communication, respect, and humility created the foundation for excellent medical care.

He provided both clinical expertise and holistic recommendations, treating us like partners in Brooke's care rather than problems to be managed. His practice set the standard for what medical relationships could be when built on mutual respect rather than institutional hierarchy.

The Balancing Act

Juggling my career and motherhood required a level of organizational skill I didn't know I possessed. My family helped when Queenie wasn't available for late work commitments or travel, but the primary responsibility was mine to navigate.

Work became complicated in new ways. Despite my proven competence and leadership during the acting supervisor role, promotions that had seemed promising suddenly became elusive. I watched colleagues I had trained or mentored advance, while I remained stagnant.

The irony wasn't lost on me—motherhood had made me more efficient, more focused, and more determined than ever. Yet somehow, having a child seemed to make me less promotable in others' eyes.

I started looking forward to going home more than advancing at work. The evening routine with Brooke—dinner, bath time, reading, rocking her to sleep—became the highlight of every day.

During the NICU months, I had lived within ten minutes of both work and the hospital, running between them like a woman possessed. I slept in hospital chairs, survived on vending machine meals, and operated on minimal self-care for nearly a year.

Home life with nursing support allowed me to breathe again. I could occasionally go to dinner alone, meet friends for coffee, and remember what it felt like to be a woman in addition to being a mother.

The nurses cleaned our house while caring for Brooke, accompanied us to appointments, and provided the buffer I needed to restore some life balance. When I worked from home, I had privacy in my office, while knowing Brooke was safe and engaged just down the hall.

Even when the balance wasn't perfect, I trusted that Jehovah wouldn't give me more than I could handle. I was built for these challenges, equipped for this purpose, strengthened by every trial we had overcome.

The Foundation We Built

Looking back on that first year home, I realize we weren't just recovering from the NICU experience—we were building the foundation for everything that would come after. Every small victory, every developmental milestone, every moment of pure joy was laying groundwork for the confident, capable person Brooke would become.

The little girl who had fought for every breath was now running through our house with boundless energy. The baby who had been fed through tubes was now painting her high chair with pureed peas and asserting her food preferences with dramatic flair.

The child who had been surrounded by machines was now creating her own soundtrack of laughter, chatter, and increasingly sophisticated demands for attention.

We had done more than survive the NICU. We had transformed trauma into triumph, fear into faith, and medical crisis into maternal confidence.

Home truly was where hope lived. And in our home, hope was flourishing beyond anything I had dared to dream during those dark months when survival was the only goal.

The victory was complete, but the journey was just beginning. And I couldn't wait to see what adventures awaited us next.

Coach's Note

THIS CHAPTER REPRESENTS THE FULL FLOWERING OF EVERYthing we fought for during those brutal NICU months. Watching Brooke claim her independence and develop her personality in the safety of our own home validated every difficult decision, every moment of advocacy, every prayer whispered in hospital corridors. The contrast between institutional care and home life revealed how much environment matters in healing and development.

- **What I needed then:** Permission to celebrate these victories without guilt, understanding that normal childhood experiences were not only possible, but inevitable.
- **What I know now:** The foundation built in those early post-NICU months—trust, joy, security—becomes the launching pad for everything that follows. Every moment of normalcy isa small miracle worth celebrating.
- **For the NICU parent reading this:** When you finally reach the point where medical needs become background noise to childhood wonder, let yourself feel the full weight of that achievement. You fought for these ordinary, extraordinary moments.

CHAPTER REFLECTIONS

1. What "ordinary" childhood moments now feel miraculous because of what you went through to reach them?

CHAPTER REFLECTIONS

2. How has your home environment supported healing and development in ways the hospital couldn't?

CHAPTER REFLECTIONS

3. What victories are you celebrating that others might not understand the significance of?

CHAPTER REFLECTIONS

4. Who have been your medical "angels" who treated you with respect and partnership rather than suspicion?

13
Watching Her Grow Beyond All Expectations

"Train up a child in the way he should go; even when he is old, he will not depart from it."
— Proverbs 22:6

The predictions had been wrong. Every single one of them.

The nurses who said she'd have developmental delays. The doctors who warned about cognitive limitations. The specialists who prepared me for a lifetime of medical interventions. As I watched Brooke command her daycare classroom like a tiny general leading her troops, I couldn't help but smile at how spectacularly they had all underestimated my daughter.

The Daycare Revolution

Since switching to the new medical team and finding our rhythm at home, Brooke had exploded beyond every expectation anyone had dared to voice. Queenie's daycare became the laboratory where Brooke's true personality finally had space to unfold, and the results were nothing short of remarkable.

Every morning, I'd drop off a child who attacked each day like it owed her something. Brooke didn't just participate in daycare activities—she revolutionized them. She took two younger children, PJ and Maya, under her wing with the authority of someone who'd survived things they couldn't imagine.

"PJ! Maya!" she'd call out when we arrived each morning, like a CEO summoning her board of directors.

The fact that both children were bigger than her didn't matter. Brooke had learned in the NICU that size had nothing to do with strength, and she carried that knowledge into every relationship. She taught them songs, showed them how to navigate playground politics, and somehow convinced them that following her lead was always the best option.

Then there was AJ, just five months older but completely mesmerized by Brooke's confident energy. Their friendship reminded me daily that some connections transcend medical history. AJ didn't care that Brooke had been born weighing less than a bag of sugar. He only knew that she was the most interesting person in the room.

"PJ! AJ!" Brooke would call out at home in the evenings, like she was summoning absent friends to continue their adventures. Her social calendar was more active than mine had ever been.

When visitors came to the daycare, Brooke transformed into the ultimate hostess—big smiles, enthusiastic hugs, and an uncanny ability to make everyone feel like they were the most important person she'd ever met. She possessed a charisma that had nothing to do with her medical journey and everything to do with who she was meant to become.

The "Fabulous and Intelligent" Diva

Queenie had become more than a daycare provider—she was Brooke's first real teacher outside of medical settings, and her observations carried weight precisely because they had no connection to hospital charts or therapeutic goals.

"Before you brought her here," Queenie told me one afternoon, "I wasn't sure what to expect based on everything you'd described. But this little girl? She's exceeding every milestone I can think of."

Brooke was eating textures that would challenge some full-term toddlers her age. She wasn't shy around strangers—quite the opposite. She approached new people with the confidence of someone who'd been surrounded by rotating medical staff her entire life and learned to win them over.

"If you didn't tell anyone she was premature, no one would ever know," Queenie observed. "She's more advanced than kids who've never seen the inside of a hospital."

It was true. Brooke's vocabulary was expanding daily, her physical coordination was remarkable, and her problem-solving skills bordered on scary. She'd figured out how to manipulate the daycare routine to her advantage, convinced other children to share their favorite toys, and somehow made herself indispensable to every activity.

"She's my fabulous and intelligent diva," Queenie would say, shaking her head with fond amazement.

The word "diva" might have been concerning in another context, but watching Brooke in action, I understood what Queenie meant. This wasn't entitled behavior—it was leadership. Brooke had learned to command attention because she'd needed advocates to survive, and now she was using those same skills to thrive.

The Support Network That Sustained Us

What struck me most during this period was how the right people had materialized at exactly the right times throughout our journey. From the NICU nurses who genuinely cared, to the home health team that treated us like family, from the doctors who respected my voice, to Queenie, who celebrated Brooke's uniqueness—each person had appeared when we needed them most.

It wasn't a coincidence. It was a confirmation that we were exactly where we were supposed to be, surrounded by exactly who we were meant to meet.

These relationships taught me patience when my natural instinct was to control every variable. They showed me that there were still good-hearted people in the world when institutional failures had made me cynical. Most importantly, they helped me feel at ease with decisions I questioned, knowing I had a network of people who truly understood what we'd been through.

"The right support comes around at the right times," I reflected one evening after a particularly good daycare report. It wasn't just true—it was evidence of divine orchestration.

Breaking Every Mold

By her second birthday, Brooke had shattered every limitation anyone had tried to place on her future. She was counting to twenty in both English and Spanish—something Queenie had taught her during their afternoon sessions. She recited her alphabet with the precision of a kindergartner and sang "Daddy Finger" every night before bed like it was a sacred ritual.

Her favorite cartoons were no longer passive entertainment—they were interactive experiences. She'd watch Bubble Guppies and anticipate every plot point, shout out answers during Super Why episodes, and dance along with Mickey Mouse with choreography she'd created herself.

But it was her social intelligence that truly amazed everyone who spent time with her. Brooke had an intuitive understanding of group dynamics that seemed far beyond her chronological age. She knew how to diffuse tension between fighting children, how to include shy kids in group activities, and how to navigate the complex politics of toddler friendships.

"She's like a little diplomat," one of the other parents observed after watching Brooke mediate a playground dispute.

The observation was more accurate than they knew. Brooke had learned negotiation skills in the NICU—how to communicate needs without language, how to work with people she didn't choose, how to persist when others wanted to give up. Those survival skills had transformed into life skills that would serve her far beyond daycare.

The Expanding Horizons

As Brooke approached her third birthday, new opportunities began presenting themselves. The physical therapy that had once been a medical necessity evolved into natural athleticism. The speech development that had been carefully monitored became effortless communication. The social skills that had been therapy goals became inherent leadership qualities.

Queenie started talking about preschool programs that might challenge Brooke academically. Other parents asked about my "secret" for raising such a confident child. Pediatricians marveled at how completely she'd overcome her premature start.

But I knew the secret wasn't really a secret at all. Brooke had been fighting since her first breath, and now that the medical battles were behind us, she was channeling that same energy into conquering childhood with remarkable enthusiasm.

The conversations at pickup shifted from medical updates to typical parenting concerns: potty training, boundary setting, preparing for eventual school transitions. These wonderfully ordinary challenges felt like victories in themselves.

"You know," Queenie said one afternoon as we watched Brooke organize a complex game involving all the daycare children, "I think you need to start thinking about what comes next for her. She's going to outgrow what I can offer here pretty soon."

The comment was both thrilling and terrifying. Outgrowing supports had always meant moving into unknown territory. But for the first time, that territory felt like an opportunity rather than a crisis.

Looking Toward Tomorrow

As we settled into our evening routine that night—dinner, bath, stories, and songs—I marveled at how far we'd traveled from those first terrifying days in the NICU. The child who'd once needed machines to breathe was now chattering nonstop about her plans for tomorrow's daycare adventures. The baby who'd been fed through tubes was now expressing sophisticated food preferences and helping me prepare simple meals. The micro-preemie who'd been too fragile to touch was now wrestling with me on the living room floor and demanding piggyback rides around the house.

Every prediction had been exceeded. Every limitation had been transcended. Every fear had been transformed into faith.

The little girl who'd defied medical odds was now defying social expectations, academic predictions, and developmental timelines with the same stubborn determination she'd shown in her isolette. She was writing her own story, and it was going to be magnificent.

As I tucked her into bed and listened to her plans for tomorrow's adventures, I realized that watching her grow beyond all expectations wasn't just about celebrating her achievements. It was about recognizing that she'd been destined for greatness from the very beginning—we'd just needed time and space for that destiny to unfold.

The NICU had been about keeping her alive. Home had been about helping her thrive. But this next phase? This was about watching her soar.

Brooke wasn't just surviving anymore—she was preparing to take on the world. And based on what I'd witnessed over the past few months, the world had better be ready for her.

Coach's Note

This phase of Brooke's development revealed something profound: the same determination that had helped her survive the NICU was now propelling her to excel in every area of childhood. The medical challenges that could have defined her limitations instead became the foundation for remarkable resilience and leadership skills.

- **What I needed then:** Confirmation that all our fighting and advocacy had actually paid off in tangible ways that others could see and celebrate.
- **What I know now:** Children who overcome early challenges often develop capacities that exceed what their peers naturally possess. The struggle becomes their strength.
- **For the NICU parent reading this:** When your child starts exceeding expectations rather than just meeting them, let yourself feel the full pride of that achievement. They're not just "catching up"—they're leading the way.

CHAPTER REFLECTIONS

1. What abilities has your child developed that seem to stem directly from their early challenges?

CHAPTER REFLECTIONS

2. How has your child's social development surprised you or others?

CHAPTER REFLECTIONS

3. What predictions about your child's future have been proven completely wrong?

CHAPTER REFLECTIONS

4. Who are the people in your support network who see your child's potential rather than their history?

The School Years Begin

"For I know the plans I have for you," declares the Lord, "plans to prosper you and not to harm you, to give you hope and a future."
— JEREMIAH 29:11

THE TRANSITION FROM DAYCARE TO FORMAL EDUCATION FELT like watching Brooke step onto a stage she'd been rehearsing for her entire life. All those months of proving doctors wrong, of exceeding medical expectations, of leading her little pack at Queenie's—it had all been preparation for this moment when she'd finally get to show the world what a micro-preemie could really accomplish.

But life had another curveball waiting for us, one that would test everything we'd built in Texas and challenge us to start over in ways I never expected.

Kindergarten: The Academic Debut

Brooke's entry into kindergarten was nothing short of triumphant. The little girl who'd once been fed through tubes was now reading at levels that amazed her teachers. The baby who'd struggled to gain weight was now a sturdy, confident five-year-old who attacked learning with the same determination she'd brought to every other challenge.

Her teachers quickly recognized that they weren't dealing with a typical student. Brooke approached academics like she'd approached recovery—with focused intensity and an almost competitive drive to exceed expectations. Reading wasn't just about recognizing words; it was about devouring stories and asking questions that revealed comprehension far beyond her grade level.

Math became a game she was determined to win. Art projects turned into elaborate productions that required the full attention of everyone around her. Even playground dynamics fell under her natural leadership, as she organized games and mediated disputes with the same diplomatic skills she'd honed in daycare.

"She's remarkable," her kindergarten teacher told me during our first conference. "I've never seen a child approach learning with such confidence and enthusiasm. Whatever you've done to prepare her, it's working."

I smiled, thinking about all the "preparation" Brooke had received in the NICU. Ten months of fighting for every milestone, of proving she was stronger than anyone expected, of learning that persistence pays off—that had been her real curriculum.

The First Grade Victory Lap

By first grade, Brooke wasn't just succeeding—she was setting the standard. Her teachers remained consistent from kindergarten, which created stability that allowed her true academic gifts to flourish. These educators understood her history without being limited by it, celebrating her achievements while maintaining appropriate expectations.

The school became our extended family in ways that reminded me of the positive relationships we'd built with our post-NICU medical team. I was on a first-name basis with the principal, volunteered for field trips, and even spoke at career day about federal government work. This wasn't just Brooke's school—it was our community.

Prince George's County public schools get a bad reputation in some circles, but our experience was nothing short of exceptional. The family-oriented atmosphere, the dedicated teachers, the genuine investment in each child's success—it all felt like vindication for every difficult decision we'd made to get to this point.

Brooke scored high on standardized tests, but more importantly, she was happy. She made two best friends—relationships that felt significant not just because they were her first real peer friendships, but because they were based on who she was now, not where she'd come from.

These girls and their mothers became part of our chosen family. We made a pact to keep the children together as much as possible, understanding that friendships like theirs were rare treasures worth protecting.

The Social Butterfly Emerges

Beyond academics, Brooke was developing into a force of nature socially. Her natural charisma, honed during those daycare years, translated beautifully into the elementary school environment. She could walk into any room and quickly identify who needed a friend, who needed a leader, and who needed someone to listen.

But she was also learning that not every social situation was as straightforward as the controlled environment we'd carefully constructed around her early years. There were mean kids, evolving playground politics, and the kinds of interpersonal challenges that couldn't be solved with the diplomatic skills she'd mastered among younger children.

We enrolled her in taekwondo, thinking martial arts would build her physical confidence and give her tools for handling conflict. The dojo became another stage for Brooke to display her determination, as she progressed through belt levels with the same methodical approach she brought to everything else.

"She's got natural talent," her instructor observed, "but more importantly, she's got heart. You can't teach that kind of fighting spirit."

I laughed to myself, thinking about how right he was. Brooke's fighting spirit had been forged in circumstances he couldn't imagine, tested in ways most children would never face, and strengthened by victories that had nothing to do with martial arts.

The taekwondo experience also introduced her to children from different schools and backgrounds, expanding her social circle beyond our immediate community. She made friends with kids who knew nothing about her medical history, who saw only her confidence and competence.

But it also exposed her to her first real experience with bullying. A former friend from gymnastics, someone who'd once been part of their tight-knit group, began targeting Brooke and her friends out of jealousy over their close relationship.

Watching my daughter navigate that situation—learning when to fight back, when to seek help, when to simply walk away—felt like watching her apply every lesson she'd ever learned about persistence, diplomacy, and self-advocacy.

The Big Decision

Just as we were settling into our Texas rhythm, life threw us another curve. I received a promotion offer that would require relocating back to the DC area—a senior advisory position that represented a significant career advancement, but would mean leaving everything we'd built.

The decision felt impossibly complex. Texas had been our healing place, our fresh start, our proof that we could build a beautiful life from the ashes of medical trauma. Brooke was thriving in school, we had strong community connections, and our support systems were firmly established.

But the opportunity was too significant to ignore. Not just in terms of career advancement, but for what it represented—validation that my years of advocacy, leadership, and persistence had been recognized at the highest levels of government service.

More practically, it would bring us closer to extended family and give Brooke the chance to develop relationships with cousins and relatives who'd only been distant voices on phone calls during her early years.

The 26-hour drive from Texas to Maryland felt both eternal and too short. Brooke cried as we finished loading the moving truck, saying, "Mom, I want to go back in my house," with a heartbreak that mirrored my own.

"No, Brooke, we're leaving and won't come back here," I told her, trying to sound more confident than I felt.

She cried herself to sleep in the car, then settled into the adventure with the resilience that had defined her entire life. On the road trip, she became my copilot, asking "Mom, are we there yet?" with increasing frequency, but also watching the changing scenery with the curiosity that made every experience a learning opportunity.

New Beginnings in Familiar Territory

The transition back to the DC area was smoother than I'd dared to hope. We stayed with relatives and my best friend while searching for our own place, and Brooke adapted to the temporary living situation with grace. She enjoyed having more people in the house, made fast friends with my best friend's son, and treated the whole experience like an extended sleepover.

Finding the right daycare became the first priority. I needed a program that would close at reasonable hours, provide solid academic preparation, and understand that Brooke needed intellectual challenges along with social development.

The Christian daycare we found was perfect—a provider with more than thirty years of experience who incorporated faith-based learning with rigorous academic standards. The curriculum was fast-paced, the staff reminded me of the warm, no-nonsense teachers I'd grown up with, and the moral foundation felt like exactly what Brooke needed as she navigated new environments.

"The classes are high-paced, and my new friends are welcoming," became Brooke's standard report about her days. She loved the structured environment, the academic challenges, and the clear expectations about behavior and character.

The teachers reminded me of the aunties I'd grown up with in the '80s—loving but firm, supportive but demanding, and committed to bringing out the best in every child. Her primary teacher became a lasting friend, someone who saw Brooke's potential immediately and nurtured it with the skill of someone who'd dedicated her life to childhood education.

The principal and school staff were equally impressive, creating a family atmosphere that made both Brooke and me feel welcomed and valued. The structure was wonderful, the discipline was consistent, and the love was evident in every interaction.

When Brooke had a speaking part in her pre-K graduation, I felt tears watching her confidently address the audience. Here was the child who'd once been so fragile that doctors questioned whether she'd survive, now commanding a stage with poise that would make any parent proud.

The Christian Academy Challenge

Our next educational step was a private Christian academy that promised to build on the foundation that the daycare had established. The school had dedicated staff, committed teachers, and an academic program that would challenge Brooke's growing capabilities.

Brooke thrived in this environment. The high-paced classes matched her learning style perfectly, and her new friends embraced her with the kind of acceptance that makes childhood friendships precious. She attended parties, participated in school events, and developed a close-knit group of friends who appreciated her leadership and humor.

Financial pressures eventually forced us to make the difficult decision to transition to public education, but not before Brooke's teacher assured me that she'd be successful wherever she went.

"She can make friends with anyone," her teacher told me. "She has the kind of personality that adapts to any environment and makes it better."

Those words felt like prophecy as we prepared for another transition. Brooke had proven over and over that she could not only survive change, but transform it into opportunity.

The Public School Triumph

The public elementary school we chose continued Brooke's streak of educational success. Her kindergarten and first-grade teachers were the same, providing the consistency that allowed her to build deep, trusting relationships with educators who understood her capabilities.

These teachers became some of our biggest advocates, celebrating Brooke's achievements while maintaining the high expectations that kept her growing. They saw her as a bright, capable student who happened to have an interesting backstory.

Brooke scored high on standardized tests, but more importantly, she was developing the kind of character and confidence that would serve her throughout life. She was learning to navigate social situations, advocate for herself academically, and build friendships based on mutual respect and shared interests.

The two best friends she made during this period became like sisters to her. Their mothers and I developed strong relationships built on our commitment to supporting these special friendships. We'd seen how rare it was for children to find genuine connections, and we were determined to nurture these bonds.

The Circle of Growth

As I watched Brooke navigate each new educational environment with increasing confidence and success, I reflected on how far we'd both traveled since those early NICU days. The little girl who'd once been connected to machines was now connecting with peers, teachers, and communities in ways that enriched everyone around her.

Her academic success felt like vindication for every difficult decision we'd made, every system we'd fought, every prediction we'd refused to accept. But more than that, it felt like confirmation that we'd been right to believe in possibilities that others couldn't see.

Brooke wasn't just meeting educational milestones—she was setting new standards for what a child with her history could achieve. She was writing her own story, and it was turning out to be even more remarkable than I'd dared to dream.

Each school transition had tested our resilience and adaptability, but they'd also revealed strengths we didn't know we possessed. We were building a foundation that would support whatever challenges and opportunities lay ahead.

The journey from Texas to Maryland had been about more than changing addresses. It had been about proving that home isn't a place—it's the strength and love you carry with you wherever you go.

And as I watched Brooke thrive in each new environment, I knew we'd be ready for whatever adventure came next.

Coach's Note

Educational transitions can be especially challenging for children with complex medical histories, but they can also be opportunities to prove that past challenges don't define future potential. Watching Brooke excel academically, while building genuine friendships, validated every difficult decision we'd made to prioritize her development over medical predictions.

- **What I needed then:** Confidence that changing environments wouldn't disrupt the progress we'd worked so hard to achieve, and faith that Brooke's resilience would translate into new settings.
- **What I know now:** Children who overcome early challenges often develop adaptability skills that serve them throughout life. The strength that helped them survive medical crises becomes the foundation for thriving in any environment.
- **For the NICU parent reading this:** When your child starts excelling in "normal" settings like school, let yourself feel the full pride of that achievement. Their success is proof that your advocacy and love created possibilities that pessimistic predictions couldn't imagine.

CHAPTER REFLECTIONS

1. How has your child's educational experience compared to the predictions made during their medical journey?

CHAPTER REFLECTIONS

2. What environments have brought out the best in your child's natural abilities?

CHAPTER REFLECTIONS

3. How do you balance protecting your child from challenges with allowing them to develop independence?

CHAPTER REFLECTIONS

4. What friendships or community connections have been most meaningful in your child's development?

Champions in the Making

*"She is clothed with strength and dignity;
she can laugh at the days to come."*
— PROVERBS 31:25

THE GIRL WHO'D ONCE FOUGHT FOR EVERY BREATH WAS NOW running track with medals around her neck. The baby who'd been fed through tubes was now confidently ordering her favorite foods at restaurants. The micro-preemie who'd defied every medical prediction was now defying athletic expectations with the same determined spirit.

As I watched eight-year-old Brooke cross the finish line at her second developmental track meet, javelin medal gleaming in the afternoon sun, I marveled at how completely our lives had transformed from those dark NICU days into something I'd never dared to dream.

The Second Grade Challenge

Our move to Charles County had brought new opportunities, but also fresh challenges. The school system was reportedly more rigorous than our previous district, and I worried about how Brooke would adapt to yet another educational environment.

Those concerns proved unfounded. Brooke finished first grade with honor roll recognition and approached second grade with the confidence of someone who'd never met an academic challenge she couldn't conquer. Her new teacher seemed nervous during our first meeting—an older educator who'd come out of retirement to handle this generation of inquisitive, tech-savvy children.

"She called Brooke a little boy and seemed extremely flustered," I noted after our initial conference. The teacher's uncertainty was immediately apparent, and I wondered if this would be our first real mismatch.

But Brooke had developed remarkable adaptability skills over the years. She'd learned to size up new environments quickly, identify the key players, and adjust her approach accordingly. Within weeks, she'd figured out her teacher's methods and found her place among her new classmates.

The real test came with the social dynamics. Being the new kid in an established classroom is challenging for any child, but Brooke had learned to navigate complex interpersonal situations during her daycare and NICU experiences. She approached friendship-building with the same strategic thinking she brought to academics.

"Some of the kids were testing me at first," she reported after her first week, "but I think they like me now."

By the end of the school year, she was not only academically successful, but had been selected for the school's science debate team—an honor typically reserved for older students. Soon she'd be confidently presenting scientific arguments to audiences of peers and parents.

The Athletic Awakening

It was during this period that we discovered Brooke's natural athletic abilities. What had started as after-school childcare at a local gymnastics facility quickly revealed itself as something much more significant.

"She's remarkably athletic," her coach observed after just a few sessions. "Her coordination, her fearlessness, her determination—these aren't things we can teach. She has natural talent."

Watching Brooke attack gymnastics routines with the same intensity she'd brought to recovery milestones felt like watching destiny unfold. The core strength that had helped her breathe independently was now powering her through complex athletic maneuvers. The determination that had carried her through medical procedures was now driving her to perfect her form on beam and floor.

But it was track and field that truly captured her imagination. When the community center offered a youth program, Brooke begged to try it. Her best friend was already participating, which provided the social motivation she needed to commit fully.

"I want to run fast like the big kids," she announced, and within weeks, she was doing exactly that.

Her coaches were amazed by her natural speed and her coachable spirit. But what impressed them most was her competitive drive—not the destructive kind that creates poor sports, but the constructive determination to improve her own performance with each practice.

The first medal came at her second track meet, in javelin—an event that required the kind of focused concentration and precise technique that Brooke had been developing her entire life. As she stood on the podium, medal hanging around her neck, I thought about all the people who'd once questioned whether she'd even walk normally.

"Mom, I want to keep doing this," she told me afterward, clutching her medal like the treasure it was.

The Taekwondo Politics

Our taekwondo journey had been positive for nearly a year, providing Brooke with physical confidence and mental discipline while giving us a reliable after-school activity. The original dojo had honored her previous training and advancement, celebrating her progress through the belt system with appropriate recognition.

But when we moved to Charles County, we had to find a new facility. The new dojo's approach was immediately problematic. Despite documentation of Brooke's previous training and belt achievements, they insisted she start over at white belt and pay for advancement levels she'd already earned.

"We'll need to call her previous dojo to verify her training," they kept saying, but those calls never seemed to happen. Meanwhile, they were happy to collect monthly fees while keeping her at beginner levels.

"She doesn't retain her lessons well," became their standard excuse when I questioned the lack of advancement.

The assessment was laughably wrong. Brooke retained everything—medical information, academic concepts, athletic techniques, social dynamics. Her memory and processing skills had been honed by years of adapting to new situations and mastering complex information quickly.

What they really meant was that she wasn't advancing at the pace that maximized their revenue stream. The business model seemed designed to keep students paying monthly fees for as long as possible, regardless of their actual skill development.

After several months of marking time at levels she'd already mastered, Brooke told me, "This doesn't feel right." Her instincts were as sharp as mine when it came to recognizing systems that prioritized profit over progress.

We left the dojo and found gymnastics and track programs that celebrated advancement and rewarded genuine achievement. The contrast was immediate and striking—coaches who wanted to see athletes improve rather than financial managers disguised as martial arts instructors.

The Writing Journey Begins

While Brooke was discovering her athletic gifts, I was uncovering my own creative potential in unexpected ways. A former colleague approached me about contributing to a collaborative book project—something that had never been on my radar, but felt intriguingly aligned with my growing desire to help other women navigate challenges.

Women of Virtue: Walking in Excellence became my introduction to the world of inspirational writing. Contributing my story about workplace harassment and personal resilience felt like a natural extension of the advocacy skills I'd developed during Brooke's medical journey.

The experience of seeing my words in print, of knowing that other women might find strength in my experiences, ignited something I hadn't anticipated. Writing became a way to process not just our NICU journey, but all the challenges and triumphs that had shaped our lives.

The second project, *Girl Get Up and Win Everyday*, allowed me to explore themes of female empowerment and resilience with even greater depth. Each writing collaboration connected me with like-minded women who understood that our struggles could become sources of strength for others.

"You have a gift for this," one of my co-authors told me. "Your voice is authentic and powerful. You should keep writing."

The suggestion planted seeds for future projects, including the book I was beginning to envision about our NICU experience. Brooke's story deserved to be told not just for our own healing, but for the families who might find hope in reading about our journey from crisis to triumph.

The Dating Dilemma

Balancing single motherhood with career advancement and personal fulfillment remained an ongoing challenge. Dating felt like navigating a complex obstacle course—finding men who could appreciate both my independence and my devotion to Brooke, who understood that we were a package deal, who brought value to our already rich life rather than complications.

"I'm looking for someone who steps up and shows genuine interest the way I need him to show up for me," I reflected during one of many conversations with friends about the dating scene.

So far, none had been able to meet that standard. The men I encountered seemed either intimidated by my strength or dismissive of my priorities. They wanted the benefits of having a relationship without understanding the responsibilities of joining a family unit—one that had already proven its resilience and success.

"Any man who comes into our lives has to be a genuine person," I reminded myself regularly. The standards weren't negotiable—Brooke and I had worked too hard to build our peaceful, purposeful life to compromise it for anything less than extraordinary love.

In the meantime, I focused on modeling independence and strength for my daughter while remaining open to the possibility that the right partner might eventually appear. But I was no longer willing to settle for companionship that didn't enhance our already fulfilling existence.

The Career Advancement

My federal career had taken remarkable turns since those early days of juggling NICU visits with work responsibilities. The promotion that brought us back to the DC area represented not just professional advancement, but validation that the leadership skills I'd developed through advocacy and crisis management were valued at the highest levels.

Working in Southwest DC, just minutes from the Smithsonian museums, felt like a daily reminder of how far we'd traveled from those uncertain Texas beginnings. The commute was manageable, the responsibilities were engaging, and the recognition was deeply satisfying.

"I serve in a senior advisory capacity now," I could say with pride, knowing that every challenge I'd overcome—medical, financial, systemic—had contributed to the expertise I brought to this role.

The balance between career ambition and motherhood had found its rhythm. I was no longer trying to prove I could do everything; I was confidently doing what mattered most, while excelling in areas that utilized my unique combination of skills and experiences.

The Champion Emerges

By age eight, Brooke had become exactly what I'd always believed she could be—not *despite* her premature start, but *because* of everything that experience had taught her about persistence, resilience, and refusing to accept limitations.

She was academically gifted, socially confident, and athletically talented. But more than that, she was kind, funny, and fiercely loyal to the people she loved. The compassion that had been nurtured during her own vulnerable period now extended to classmates who needed friendship, teammates who needed encouragement, and family members who needed her infectious optimism.

"She's like a little diplomat," observers continued to note, watching her navigate complex social situations with wisdom beyond her years.

Her athletic achievements were mounting—medals in track, recognition in gymnastics, and coaches who saw unlimited potential in her combination of natural ability and competitive spirit. But what impressed me most was her attitude toward both victory and disappointment.

"I did my best" became her standard response to any outcome, win or lose. The child who'd fought for every breath had learned that effort mattered more than results, that improvement was more valuable than perfection, that showing up was always the first step toward success.

The Reminder

The writing projects had connected me with women who understood the power of turning pain into purpose. Each collaboration reinforced my belief that our NICU journey—as difficult as it had been—was meant to become a source of hope for other families facing similar challenges.

"You should write your own book," multiple co-authors suggested. "Your story could help so many people."

The idea was taking shape, fueled by conversations with other NICU parents who felt isolated in their experiences and hungry for resources that addressed not just medical needs but emotional survival.

The Present Moment

As I write this, Brooke is thriving in ways that continue to surprise and delight everyone who knows her. She approaches each day with infectious enthusiasm, tackles challenges with inspiring confidence, and treats relationships with unshakeable loyalty.

Our life isn't perfect—we still face the normal challenges of single parenthood, academic pressures, social navigation, and future planning. But we face them from a foundation of strength that was forged in the crucible of medical crisis and tempered by years of proving that love, determination, and faith can overcome any obstacle.

The little girl who once weighed barely over a pound now carries herself with the confidence of someone who knows she can handle whatever life brings. The baby who doctors weren't sure would survive is now setting goals for high school athletics and dreaming about college possibilities.

The scared new mother who felt overwhelmed by medical complexity has become a confident advocate who helps other women find their voices and claim their power. The woman who once questioned whether she deserved motherhood now mentors others through their own seasons of doubt and growth.

We've built something beautiful from something terrifying. We've transformed trauma into triumph, fear into faith, and medical crisis into life celebration.

And this is just the beginning.

The champions we've become—both individually and together—are ready for whatever adventures await us. We've proven that "premature" doesn't mean limited, that different doesn't mean less, that challenging beginnings can lead to extraordinary outcomes.

Brooke's medals are lovely, but they're just external recognition of internal qualities that were developed long before she ever stepped onto a track. Her academic achievements are wonderful, but they're just proof of intellectual gifts that were nurtured through years of overcoming obstacles.

Our real victory isn't in any single accomplishment—it's in the daily reality of a life lived fully, purposefully, and joyfully, despite a beginning that could have defined us as limited or damaged.

We are champions, not because we won a particular battle, but because we learned how to fight with grace, how to persevere with hope, and how to transform every challenge into an opportunity for growth.

The NICU made us survivors. Everything that came after made us champions.

And our championship season is just getting started.

Coach's Note

This phase of our journey represents the full flowering of everything we fought for during those brutal early years. Watching Brooke excel—not just academically, but athletically and socially—while I found my own voice as a writer and advocate felt like watching multiple dreams come true simultaneously. We'd proven that trauma could become the foundation for triumph.

- **What I needed then:** Confirmation that the foundation we'd built was strong enough to support not just survival but true flourishing in multiple areas of life.
- **What I know now:** The skills children develop overcoming early challenges often translate into exceptional capabilities in unexpected areas. The same determination that helped Brooke survive the NICU now powers her athletic achievements and academic success.
- **For the NICU parent reading this:** Your child's challenges are developing capacities that will serve them throughout life. The strength you're building together will become the foundation for achievements you can't yet imagine.

CHAPTER REFLECTIONS

1. What unexpected talents or interests has your child discovered as they've grown?

CHAPTER REFLECTIONS

2. How have the skills you developed during crisis periods served you in other areas of life?

CHAPTER REFLECTIONS

3. What dreams are you allowing yourself to pursue, now that the survival phase is behind you?

CHAPTER REFLECTIONS

4. How do you balance protecting your child's achievements while encouraging continued growth and challenge-taking?

Survival Tips for NICU Families

> *"The Lord your God is with you, the Mighty Warrior who saves. He will take great delight in you; in His love, he will no longer rebuke you, but will rejoice over you with singing."*
> — Zephaniah 3:17

This experience was still difficult at times to explain since Brooke's condition was so rare. I developed some practical survival tips that I followed on a daily basis to keep my head clear and focused on positive outcomes. Some things that I did were pray, read/verbally repeat positive affirmations, talk to my mother, and focus on a hobby or activities that reminded me of who I was. Lastly, I set aside days that I called "Lady Time." These were days when I went to the nail or beauty salon. It was very therapeutic, and I believe that I deserve to be pampered on occasion.

Seek Spiritual Guidance

My spiritual guidance came from more than Bible scriptures, meditation, and reading. I also sought solace from motivational speakers such as T.D.

Jakes, Nicole Mason, and Shanel Cooper-Sykes, to name a few. Their speeches and lectures of encouragement helped me make it through times when I was disappointed in the answers that the doctors were unable to provide. I understood that sometimes it went beyond medical advice, and I knew that Brooke's will, determination, and strength were enough. I just had to be patient and allow faith to work. I was humbled to learn patience. I asked through prayer and silent meditation while my mind was at ease.

I also started carrying crystals with me. The crystals symbolized different moods and emotions that soothed my soul. I found a quiet space and often just let my mind be clear of all of the clutter that involved the doctors, work, or life in general. I believe that you must be at peace with the mind to fully see the big picture. Too much mess becomes a distraction and could cause focus to be lost or missed.

I also prayed as often as I could. I learned from Shanel Cooper-Sykes to stay confident, poised, and positioned to not only ask, but be clear and unafraid to ask, what I needed God to fulfill. Throughout this journey, I asked God to heal my daughter's heart so that she might function better than normal and see life fully, live as she wanted, and be who she truly was. I asked for an abundance of resources and to have everything that would allow for a great lifestyle. Through prayer, I felt clear and purposeful about my intentions and motivated to move forward each day.

I ask that you do a small exercise. Take a deep breath and ask yourself:

What is it that motivates me when times are hard? Do I believe that there is more beyond what I see every day? What are some things that I can do to add spiritual value to my life?

Research

Research became an imperative part of our journey. It wasn't until I asked questions, read medical journals, and started constantly asking doctors for results that some actions happened in the NICU. I was given little to no information about Brooke's condition until I decided to research it myself.

I began questioning each plan of care for Brooke after the PDA ligation procedure. She still continued to breathe quickly after this surgery, so I started reading medical journals about babies in similar conditions. I also took some articles for the doctor to review, which led to more in-depth discussions about her condition and what the next steps would be. Those honest discussions felt so much more productive.

There were organizations that educated people about pulmonary hypertension. The Pulmonary Hypertension Association was a great resource for me. The condition happened more to adults than children, but preterm babies with this condition were increasingly becoming more commonplace in the NICU. There was no known cure. The condition was progressive and could be treated with medication. A person could have short-term or long-term effects depending on where they were on the low- to high-risk scale of symptoms.

Seek More Medical Opinions

The moment I suggested that Brooke be removed from the NICU to another hospital, she suddenly became too sick to move. But after she was discharged, I could take her to another doctor of my choice for another medical opinion. I showed an electronic medical record to a cardiologist. He said that all things done had been good practices to treat her condition.

I took her to another hospital to complete her care. After seeking a second opinion, Brooke was found to have no traces of pulmonary hypertension. I was thankful that I was able to get the second opinion so that I could proceed with her care with a new direction.

I also took her to one of the top pulmonologists in the Dallas-Fort Worth area. He was very brilliant and had great reviews among parents as well as my nursing staff company. Brooke was even smiling with him on her first visit. He came with more knowledge than I had seen about pulmonary hypertension and was very attentive when I explained Brooke's case. He agreed to take over her care and began prescribing her medications.

If you need to get a second, third, or fourth opinion, go ahead. We owe it to our children to get the proper care and advice from doctors.

Attend NICU Meetings

Often, there were support groups that worked directly with hospital NICUs. In these meetings, many NICU parents were present. Some spoke, while others listened. Activities were planned almost daily, like basket weaving, painting, CPR classes, and couples' movies.

Attending these support groups meant connecting on a level you might not expect. The meetings weren't just about shared grief; they were about celebrating every moment, no matter how small. But more than that, they were also a great way to network and build a genuine connection with parents who shared a similar story—a connection that lasts.

Find Support

Having support was really important. For me, most of my cheerleaders were friends and family, but I also had to be careful what I chose to listen to. The positive advice was great, of course. Sometimes people, even family, may not understand exactly how you feel, and may say things that you have to ignore.

Support could also come from your coworkers. My coworkers donated a total of 310 hours for me to be at home with Brooke. That touched me greatly. I had always been a supportive coworker when I could, so this really showed me how much they valued me. Brooke and I had enough hours to spend together thanks to the donated time from my coworkers.

Social media was also therapeutic for me. My Facebook community was supportive and gave me some kind words of inspiration. Some of my new friends also had premature babies and shared their experience. I eventually created a website to blog about Brooke's experience, which itself became its own community for other NICU parents.

Seek Positive Solace

I can't count how many times doctors and nurses debated with me about Brooke's care. I had to be her advocate because they exaggerated and even made her condition sound worse than it was. I was told that she was not going to make it. There were people at that hospital making a case against me as a mother. There will be tough days, and days when everything seems too overwhelming to handle.

But you can. Keep reminding yourself of that. You can handle this.

Positive affirmations did a lot of the heavy lifting for me. I gave myself pep talks whenever I could, and I went in frequently to talk to Brooke as well. I told her that she was gonna be just fine and to continue to be the strong, resilient, and exuberant baby that she was. She always smiled when I told her things like that. I think it really helped both of us.

Find Your Passion

Immerse yourself in your passions. Whether writing, drawing, meditating, or socializing, I always made time for my self-preservation. You are an important asset to yourself and your family. Your happiness and fulfillment will help you be the best you can be for them. You may find that your passion leads to a valuable network of like-minded people, or even an additional income. Ultimately, you must surround yourself with what you expect from the future.

Seek Some Light

There was always light at the end of the tunnel. Even with the unanswered questions from Brooke's line of specialty doctors, I saw massive improvements in her condition. Her oxygenation levels went from ninety-five to one-hundred percent seemingly overnight. She had no more traces of pulmonary hypertension. Behaviorally, she was a normal baby, talking, standing, playing, pitching a fit, and making silly noises. She was a happy little girl who continued to be active, grow, and love all of the attention that she got from her mother.

It was a long road to get where we are. I would not wish this on any parent, especially a first-time mother. This was not what I had first envisioned for Brooke or myself. But I wouldn't trade this, or her, for anything in the world.

God makes no mistakes. I am so happy to be able to share my experience. God paved the path for us, and because we trust in Him, we get to celebrate our countless victories. Together.

Coach's Note

This chapter contains the hard-won wisdom I wished someone had given me on day one of our NICU journey. These weren't just survival tips—they were tools for transformation. Every strategy here was born from necessity and tested in the fire of real crisis.

- **What I needed then:** A roadmap for maintaining my sanity and strength during the longest, most uncertain period of my life.
- **What I know now:** Self-care isn't selfish when you're fighting for your child's life—it's strategic. You can't advocate on empty.
- **For the NICU parent reading this:** Pick one or two strategies that resonate with you and start there. You don't have to implement everything at once, but you do need to start somewhere.

CHAPTER REFLECTIONS

1. Which of these survival strategies speaks to your current situation most strongly?

CHAPTER REFLECTIONS

2. What would your "Lady Time" or self-care ritual look like?

CHAPTER REFLECTIONS

3. How can you create a support network, even when you feel isolated in your experience?

Faith, Fire, and the Future

"I can do all things through Christ who strengthens me."
— Philippians 4:13

Covered in Grace

The Bible verse that stays in my memory and helps me through the most challenging moments in my life is Philippians 4:13. This verse encourages me, letting me know that I am backed by God through all trials and tribulations that I face. As a single woman and mother, I know that God is with me because my faith allows me to keep pushing. Faith is a must! I have to stay strong, healthy, and sane to raise Brooke.

It gets hard, but this verse gives me the extra motivation to know that everything will be just fine and something will always work out, no matter how murky things may appear. I relax, close my eyes, and pray for the strength to be able to handle whatever the day's issues may bring. I am a constant work in progress, and I coach myself daily and tell myself, *"You got this."*

God has seen me through a broken heart, disappointment from being rejected for a promotion, and a NICU experience that would break most. No one else could possibly be the answer except God. Without Him, I wouldn't be able to breathe, live, or provide for us. It gives me comfort and relief to know that, even though I cannot physically touch God or His son Jesus, they are my protectors and will continue to guide me throughout my life.

Finding Forgiveness and Understanding

I used to feel guilty about Brooke's prematurity. That guilt had a way of creeping into my quiet moments. But over time, I knew I had to come to an understanding of her condition—one that went deeper than fear. I began researching micro-prematurity through medical journals, stories of other NICU babies, and even talking to my mother, who had walked a similar path during my own NICU stay. Nurses who were kind during Brooke's NICU journey offered encouragement and shared homeopathic remedies that brought me peace.

I became familiar with the complicated medical terms—anemia, hypothermia, cerebral palsy, respiratory distress. And every time Brooke overcame a complication, my heart sang with gratitude. My daughter defied the odds. Her smile reminded me daily: Brooke was not only surviving, she was thriving. We continue to grow together.

The Labels I Carried

I was labeled a helicopter parent—hovering, watching, questioning. But that was never my intent. I wasn't trying to control; I was trying to understand. I was trying to protect.

During our NICU stay, I often felt locked out of Brooke's care. It was like the medical staff had the answers, and I was the last to know. I would be sitting there, holding my baby, while conversations happened around me as if I were invisible. I wasn't trying to be difficult. I just wanted to be included in every step of her development. I didn't want to miss anything.

Now I understand: My vigilance wasn't a flaw. It was the fierce love of a mother determined to be an advocate. Those moments in the NICU, while traumatic, helped shape me into the strong, faithful, and determined woman I am today. It was not easy—but we made it through. And today, I don't just parent with love—I parent with power.

Building My Purpose From the Pain

After the NICU and moving into the new home, there were three endeavors I wanted to pursue: completing my voice-over certification, getting my life coach certification, and establishing my career consulting vehicle.

When I was a teen and young adult, I had a love for entertainment. I often acted in commercials or videos. I always wanted to do voice-over acting and decided to work with Such A Voice. I took a course under one of their coaches and completed my demo reel upon graduating. This is a skill I intend to use once this book is published.

I got my life coach certification because it was something that I felt I needed to do while I was going through the ups and downs of the NICU. Instead of being a victim, I wanted to help other women with their trauma. I attended the classes on weekends and successfully completed the certification. During the training, I met many serving-heart women who had stories similar to mine. After this, I knew that at some point, I could impact someone's life.

Lastly, career consulting was something I did voluntarily in my federal career. Often, my coworkers would talk to me about issues they were having with others in the workplace. I was a great listener and offered solutions that worked for most who accepted. This was natural to me.

A Final Word: Faith is the Foundation

You've walked this journey with me—from hospital walls filled with uncertainty to a home filled with Brooke's laughter and light. You've witnessed the setbacks, the prayers, the diagnoses, the milestones, and the miracles.

My story is not just about NICU survival. It is about the power of resilience. It's about confronting heartbreak, enduring trials, and leaning on faith even when it feels like everything is falling apart. It's about rising—over and over again. I wrote this for every mother who has felt helpless. For every woman who's had to fight for her child. For every person navigating grief, anxiety, rejection, or disappointment.

You are not alone.

Through faith, we found light in the darkest of tunnels. Through faith, I learned to forgive the past, embrace the present, and believe in a future so much greater than I imagined. And through faith, I now stand here not only as Brooke's mother—but as a voice of strength, an advocate for healing, and a beacon of hope.

Let my journey be your reminder:

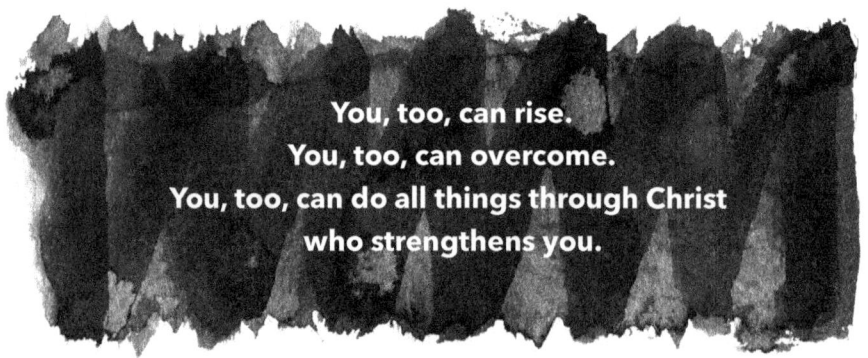

A Letter to the NICU Parent Holding On

If you're reading this from a hospital room, from a pumping station at two o'clock in the morning, or from the parking lot where you just cried until you couldn't anymore—this letter is for you.

I see you. I see you showing up when your body is still healing. I see you learning medical terms you never wanted to know. I see you being strong when you feel like breaking. I see you loving a baby you might be afraid to touch. You are doing better than you think. Your questions matter. Your instincts are valid. Your presence is medicine your baby needs.

It's okay to be scared. It's okay to be angry. It's okay to feel guilty or lost or overwhelmed. But don't you dare feel alone. There's a community of us who walked this path before you, and we're cheering you on from the other side.

Your story isn't over. It's just beginning.

Hold on.

Coach's Note

If you're reading this final chapter, I want to personally thank you for walking with me through one of the most intimate and challenging seasons of my life. Sharing Brooke's story, and mine, was not easy—but it was necessary. My hope is that, as you've turned each page, you've found pieces of your own strength reflected back at you.

This journey has taught me more about faith, resilience, and surrender than I ever imagined. And if there's anything I want you to remember as you close this book, it's this: *You are stronger than you think.* Your faith—however fragile it may feel on some days—is the foundation that can carry you through anything.

As your coach, I want to offer you these final reflections:

- Your story matters. Don't be afraid to speak it, live it, and share it. There is power in your voice.
- Your healing is a journey. It may take time, and that's okay. Every tear, every prayer, every step forward counts.
- You are never alone. Even when it feels like no one understands, trust that God sees you. He is walking with you, strengthening you in ways you can't always see.
- Be your own advocate. Whether you're navigating motherhood, health challenges, relationships, or career changes—speak up. Trust your instincts. You have wisdom for a reason.

- Celebrate your wins. Big or small, every victory is a sign of your growth. Brooke's first steps were mine, too. Her laughter is my healing.

This book may end here, but your story continues. I pray you walk boldly into your next chapter—armed with faith, courage, and the knowledge that you were built for this.

With love and light,
Kristee

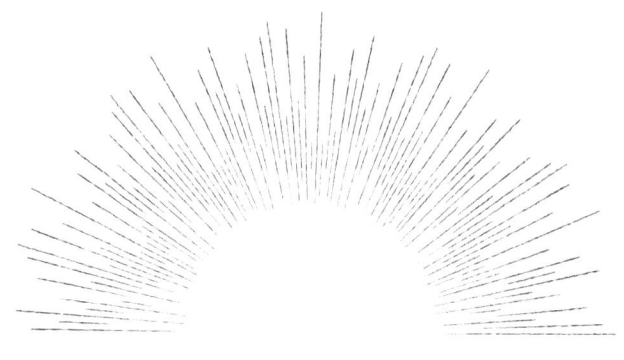

Resource Links for NICU Families

National Organizations

March of Dimes—NICU Family Support® Program
A program that helps parents during their NICU journey by providing education, staff training, and emotional support: https://www.marchofdimes.org/our-work/nicu-family-support

National Association of Neonatal Nurses (NANN)
A professional organization offering neonatal nursing resources and education: https://www.nann.org/
   For general info on neonatal nursing, see also related resources like the Academy of Neonatal Nursing: https://www.academyonline.org/

Hand to Hold

Provides early intervention mental health aid for NICU families through support groups, peer mentoring, counseling, and more: https://handtohold.org/

Graham's Foundation

Offers emotional support, resources, and community for families of micro-preemies. Includes the MyPreemie app for parents: http://www.grahamsfoundation.org

Online Communities

NICU Central

A supportive online space for NICU parents to connect: https://www.facebook.com/NICUCentral

Preemie Parent Alliance

Another peer-to-peer community; commonly linked via NICU support websites: https://www.youtube.com/channel/UCJ8yMZ5-IQ_zSMAxKF056ug

The Smallest Things

Offers stories and support for NICU families: https://www.thesmallestthings.org

Books for Further Reading

- *The Preemie Parent's Survival Guide to the NICU*—A practical resource for navigating the NICU experience.
- *Micro Preemie Memoir*—A first-person story of surviving as an extremely premature baby.

Continue the Journey

CONNECT WITH KRISTEE

About the Author

KRISTEE HALL IS A MOTHER, ADVOCATE, AND FAITH-CENTERED life coach whose life was transformed by her daughter Brooke's premature birth and extended stay in the NICU. What began as a season of fear became the foundation of her purpose—to help women trust their intuition, reclaim their voice, and stand firm in faith during life's most difficult moments.

Through *Brooketales*, Kristee shares her story as both a testimony of survival and a message of hope, encouraging readers to advocate boldly, believe deeply, and walk forward with faith.

www.ingramcontent.com/pod-product-compliance
Lightning Source LLC
Chambersburg PA
CBHW051125160426
43195CB00014B/2350